Before&After
PAGE DESIGN

JOHN McWADE

Peachpit Press

Before & After Page Design
John McWade

Peachpit Press
1249 Eighth Street
Berkeley, CA 94710
510/524-2178
510/524-2221 (fax)

Find us on the World Wide Web at: **www.peachpit.com**
To report errors, please send a note to errata@peachpit.com

Peachpit Press is a division of Pearson Education

Editor: Cathy Fishel
Production Editor: Lupe Edgar
Compositor: Kim Scott
Indexer: Joy Dean Lee
Cover design: Kim Scott
Interior design: Kim Scott

Notice of Rights

Notice of Liability

Trademarks

ISBN 0-201-79537-X

9 8 7 6 5 4 3 2

Printed and bound in the United States of America

Acknowledgements

We began publishing *Before & After* magazine in 1990, and this is our first book, derived from selections from our first 34 issues. It exists because of the vision and hard work of others. I must first thank our business partner Michael Solomon, without whom we simply wouldn't be here. His contribution reminds me of 2003's thrilling Fiesta Bowl (which he attended). In the final seconds of a heroic game, Ohio State came up short on the final drive. The season ended, and Miami had won... but, but, wait... there's a flag on the field. The game is not over, the Buckeyes still live, and they have another shot. They take it, and this time they win.

That's what Michael has done for us.

Thank you to the countless *B&A* subscribers who have written to us over the years. We happily papered our walls with your letters until we ran out of wall space, and always wished we could answer every one (that would have been a full-time job). Your support has been rewarding, encouraging, incredibly strengthening. We've kept every letter.

Thank you to Chuck Donald and Andy Markley, former staff designers whose work you'll see on these pages. Thank you to Chuck Green, *Before & After*'s most talented and consistent contributor over the years.

With a smile I thank Seth Godin, whose contribution has consisted entirely of his belief in us, good advice and moral support.

To the hardworking crew at Peachpit Press, thank you *very much*—to Cathy Fishel, our editor; Kim Scott, our designer; executive editor Marjorie Baer, our liaison; Nancy Ruenzel, publisher; Lupe Edgar, production editor; and assistant editor Suzie Lowey for helping track myriad files coming and going.

And finally, thank you to my wife Gaye, who's toiled by my side for nearly 30 years—nurturing, challenging, keeping me focused, restoring my vision when I lost it—and without whom there never would have been a *Before & After* magazine.

Table of contents

Foreword

This book, like the magazine from which it is derived, has a story behind it, but I want to start with the ending, because that's the part that matters.

The ending is this: Design is not about hardware or software. Those are what get all the press, but they are only the tools, and you can buy them with money. Design is about you—what you know, what you see, and what you have to say.

No matter how sophisticated your machine, when you turn it on what you face is the same thing that creative people have always and forever faced: the blank page.

Every painter, every musician, every writer, every designer knows the feeling. Kinda scary. Kinda lost. Kinda helpless. In front of you is possibility, hope, and fear.

What will it be?

How will it look?

Where do you even begin?

Some have filled their pages with holy words, others with symphonies and sonatas. One put the Mona Lisa on his. Another, the Declaration of Independence. Before Tolkien wrote *The Lord of the Rings*, he fussed and fidgeted over a blank sheet of paper.

Disneyland began on a blank page. Skyscrapers, automobiles, every product of every kind first had to be imagined, written, designed, produced, and brought to market.

At every step of the way, that sheet of paper was first empty.

Then someone makes a mark, draws a line, spells a word, and at that instant, something becomes visible. Something that will have an effect.

What will you put on your page?

What will it achieve?

Will it have life? Will it guide or clarify or comfort? Will it instruct or inspire or entertain?

Will it make a difference? Will it matter?

It can, you know.

Design is about you—what you know, what you see, and what you have to say.

Behind every design is a vision, a purpose, a reason to be. Page design, after all, is not about decoration but communication, about making your words and vision visible, giving it form and body for all the world to see. And so, this book is about how to design a page—and not just any page, but your page. It's about how to express in a few words, a few shapes, a few colors, the ideas you want to convey.

Before & After is here to help you get there.

Introduction

I didn't start out as a designer. I started out as the publisher of a tiny street newspaper—eight pages every couple months or so. I was 20 years old. But I was aware from the start that the way the paper looked—the mix and character of its typefaces and sizes, the general rhythm of its layouts—had an effect on how readers perceived it. When the design of it was right, it was absolutely believable, solid as rock. When it was wrong, it had no presence at all, no authority; it looked like the collage of articles that it was, something any amateur could do.

It's hard to describe, but I could tell that the right design transcended the ink and paper. Designed correctly, the paper did not appear to be designed at all; what the reader perceived was power and presence. But designed incorrectly, the look became visible; it was now awkward, an impediment.

Poor design is like smog. You can see air only when it's dirty. When it's clean it's invisible and you see the fantastic mountains, unaware of the air at all.

Design is like that.

Designed correctly, my paper, small as it was, looked big, strong, *right*. That's where I discovered that design mattered—that it was not an add-on, not a frill, not an option, but part and parcel with the message.

I took art in college, but my first real job in this business was working for a printer. In 1973, Dynagraphic Printing in Reno, Nevada, was the hot shop in town, and Don Landeck hired me to do pasteup. Pasteup was the term he used for the kind of artwork that a printer did. Real art came from creative agencies; we were the pinch hitters, the subs. We did the quick, cheap stuff—business cards, fliers, class reunion brochures—for clients who didn't like, couldn't afford or hadn't the time for agency work, and often for those who just walked through the door. In a room the size of a big closet, we had at our disposal an IBM Selectric Composer, some clip-art books, a supply of rub-down lettering and a stat camera with a vacuum motor loud enough to scare burglars. Clients at this level were not especially fussy, which meant

It was great; there was plenty of pressure but miles of creative leeway.

that our design "experiments"—important in those formative years—were accepted more often than not. It was great; there was plenty of pressure but miles of creative leeway.

For the next 12 years I, like all designers, worked by hand on a drawing board, with mechanical tools—T-square, triangle, felt pens, hot wax. Typeset text would arrive set in long strips, which we would cut with scissors and paste onto paper, just like we did in kindergarten but with more precision. (When I say "we," I'm talking about my wife Gaye and me, except this was before we were married.) The "pasteups" went into a darkroom to be copied by a camera onto film, which was "stripped up" and burned onto a metal plate, which was then fastened to a press and the job printed.

Whether you go back as far as I do or your entire design experience has been digital, you'll recognize the terms. *Cut, copy, paste.* That's where they came from.

Until 1985, every job in the world was done this way. And then came the computer.

Worlds collide

In July 1985, desktop publishing changed everything. It changed the world's biggest industry overnight, completely and permanently. It changed how visual material got planned, prepared and produced. It changed the techniques, the timelines, the dynamics. Those of us in the graphic arts were swept in one incredible step from the wooden world of drawing boards and T-squares and ruling pens—the beloved horses and buggies of our craft—to the cold electronic realm of digits and pixels. Complicated, tactile work that had required big staffs and equipment and planning and coordination and expense now could be produced, start to finish, by one person at a desk with a computer. It was amazing.

For me, it had begun earlier that year, in February at a Seybold conference in Los Angeles. I was there as a guest of Scitex (electronic prepress) and had spent the afternoon designing a magazine spread at the Astra system's expensive console. Before heading home, I peered into a downstairs room full of Macintosh computers. They seemed like toys in comparison! In the corner was a man sitting transfixed by a Mac screen. I went to watch.

On his tiny screen was a block of text and an arrow. When he moved the mouse, the arrow moved. He placed the arrow atop the text—I wasn't ready for what I was about to see—and moved the text by eye as casually as if it were on paper! No codes, no special monitors, no numbered coordinates; he just moved it. The

million-dollar machine upstairs *could not do that.* I was stunned.

He was excited himself, not because the text had moved but because he had just made it *snap to a guide.* Jeremy Jaech, chief engineer of a tiny Seattle startup called Aldus, sat in that chair writing a piece of software they would be calling PageMaker. My life changed course right there.

I flew home with Jeremy's promise to send me a test copy, and told my boss that I was

In the corner was a man sitting transfixed by a Mac screen. I went to watch.

quitting the best graphics job in Sacramento to start a new business—a desktop publishing business—by myself, relying on a program that did not yet exist. I was about to make pages and test software; it sounded to me like design and laboratory work, and so I christened my microscopic company PageLab. It was the first desktop publishing business in the world.

I spent the next four months on the phone at all hours of the day and night. "Jeremy," I'd say, "PageMaker must have a hairline." "We weren't planning on that," he'd say. "It must," I'd say.

Those were the days before PageMaker would set type. On version 0.8, a line ruled beyond the page margin would crash the program with lights and loud noises—*banana-nu-nu land*, Aldus called it. Jeremy sent an engineering version containing a debugger. I'd be laying out a page when *zot!*—PageMaker would be gone, replaced by onscreen hieroglyphics. I'd phone. "What's the 19th character in the sixth line?" he'd ask. "17," I'd answer. "Great; change it to 16," he'd say. I could tell he was writing it down.

Apple Computer phoned. "We hear you're doing good things with PageMaker and we'd like to put you on videotape. Would you be up for that?" said the voice. They *helicoptered* a four-man crew to PageLab—a closet-size room (I mean it)—and filmed away. The footage became part of Apple's first desktop publishing video and was seen around the world.

Apple phoned. "Will you make pages with PageMaker for our national advertising?" I did, twice. That work got into *Time* magazine.

Apple phoned. "Will you design a poster for us?" they asked. "What would you like it to be?" I replied. "Don't know—it's for a desktop publishing forum; we hoped you'd have some ideas." I created *How to Design a Page* on Saturday and on Monday drove to Cupertino with proofs. "You did this with our computer?" they asked. I was surprised by their surprise. "No one here does this," they said. "I just used PageMaker," I said. "But you're using it," they said, "to design cool stuff."

That's where it started.

It's still cool

I call myself a designer because I make a living at it. But design doesn't belong to a particular class of people. Beauty is one of life's fundamentals, like love and laughter. It's *ours.* We're all attracted to beautiful things and repelled by ugly ones. And while we have our own artistic preferences—I like red, you like blue, and these preferences wax and wane over a lifetime—our sense of beauty is really quite common.

So is our need for it.

Our circulation manager Alan came to work one day in a pair of shoes that had me reaching for my sunglasses. Brilliant white, jet black, stripes all over, *Nike,* they said on the side. They cost $125 and outsell $50 competitors. Why? Design.

Arriving every day in our office mailbox is a thick stack of print advertising, which we sort over the wastebasket. *Junk, junk, junk, maybe, junk, junk*, and so on. How do we decide which to keep? Design.

In the '90s Ford Motor Company rolled out an important new Taurus that it had spent $2.8 billion to design. Nearly three thousand million dollars on the design of *one car*. Let that sink in.

Design has always been important, but the computer has put it center stage. Its influence on commerce is huge. It's no longer enough to have a good product; it must be a good-looking product. It's no longer enough to publish the news; it must be good-looking news. Good design sells products. Good design—beauty—moves hearts and minds and mountains.

What's all this mean for designers?

It means a lot of fun, that's what. And because it's more competitive, it means a lot of sweat.

Design has always been important, but the computer has put it center stage.

What does it take to be a designer?

1) It starts with an interest. I was going to say it starts with a love of design, but I didn't start by loving it; I started by being interested, and began to love it after I began acquiring…

2) Skills. Design can be a gratifying spectator sport, but if you're going to make it happen you need to get your hands on it, you need to get involved, you need to work with the tools.

This is what makes the computer exciting; it's a store full of tools. With it you can set type, you can draw pictures, you can work photos. You can design every aspect of every page, print it in your office, upload it to the Web and see the results in seconds. It's fantastic.

Time to make magic

Design is a language like speech and music: To master it takes practice. The nice thing is, with our magic box, practice is fun, and so we can practice a lot; we can now design everything.

To succeed as a designer it's important that you respect your need to learn. Give yourself room; there is a lot to know. I'm not telling you to stop short of the highest. But take pleasure in every small victory on the way up. Design is not a contest, and what I mean by that is you can't lose, not as long as you keep at it. You may not get this job or that, but you'll get better and better.

Give yourself room to be disappointed, too. An athlete doesn't hurdle a 7-foot-high bar on the first try. He endures a lot of days on his back with that stupid bar on his chest.

Study. Look around. Keep at it.

When I was a kid I thought there'd come a time when I would *arrive*—you know, be there. On top. And to my youthful mind, this meant being done, on cruise control, no more work.

Shows what I knew.

Life, I'm happy to report, is too big to be done. Beauty forever beckons. That's what I like best about desktop publishing.

Enjoy the book.

Newsletters & Newspapers

Beautiful and simple, too, win accolades with this one-column gem.

How to design a news *letter*

Once upon a time, *newsletter* meant an actual letter, with news. That was before desktop publishing got us making them into little newspapers, with columns and boxes and all that. Why wrestle with such complications? This sleek, letter-style design communicates better—and is *much* easier to make. Print it on nice paper, and you'll win raves—*and* get your evenings back. Here's how.

Type Note   This design uses Times for text and Futura—a very bold sans serif—for heads, captions and quotes. It is a handsome combination, but many others will do. When choosing, look for lots of contrast; the small heads need to stand out.

TIMES   FUTURA EX BOLD

1 Set up the grid

Although the text is set in one wide column, a sophisticated, six-column grid underlies the page. It is used to guide your placement of headlines, photos, captions and quotes, ensuring a neat, consistent layout.

Page specs
Here are the measurements used (in picas): a letter-size page, left margin of 13p; right margin, 9p; top margin 4p; and bottom margin, 4p. There are six columns, with one pica between each. Using your ruler guides, drag your horizontal guides to 4, 11.5, 19, 59 and 62 picas. Drag vertical guides to 2, 9 and 44 picas.

What makes it work?
Recessed headlines and bylines. One size, one width, no clutter.

Photos, quotes and text snap to vertical grid for handsome, consistent pages.

Asymmetrical page leaves room for *stuff*—a logo, list of corporate officers, newsletter staff, publication date, photos, quotes, anything.

Spacious, 18-point text leading yields high legibility, adds an elegant air. Keeps production peppy, too—it snaps right to the standard ruler.

2 Set up style sheets

Edit style			Type					Paragraph					Spacing	Hyph
Name	Based on	Next	Font	Size	Lead	Color	Case	Left	First	Right	Align	After	Letter	
Body	No style	Same	Times	10.5	18	Black	Normal	0	1	0	Just			On
Body First	Body	Body	Times	10.5	18	Black	Normal	0	0	0	Just			On
Byline	No style	Same	FutBd	6	7	Black	All caps	0	0	1	Left		40	Off
Headline	No style	Byline	FutXBd	10	12	Black	All caps	0	0	1	Left*	0p4	0	Off
Quote	No style	Same	FutXBd	7	8	White	All caps	1	1	0	Ctr			On
Caption	Quote	Same	FutXBd	7	8	Black	Normal	1	1	0	Ctr			On
Address	No style	Same	FutBd	6	15	Black	Normal	0	0	0	Left			On
Date	Address	Same	FutBd	5.5	7	Black	Normal	0	0	0	Left			On

*Add rule below paragraph: Weight: 1pt., Offset: 0p6, Length: text. Remove rule when setting remaining styles.

3 Build the nameplate

The nameplate relies on a bold, condensed typestyle for its visual muscle; the font used here is Onyx. Note that the condensed characters, normally used to save space, have here been spread apart. This visual counterpoint gives the nameplate its unique style. To do this, *force-justify* the name to the ends of the bars beneath. To look as if you've worked harder, set the first letter bigger, in a separate text block, and stretch the others to meet it. Then align the tops as shown; note where the finished word rests on the gray bars. The white subtitle is also force justified within the gray bar.

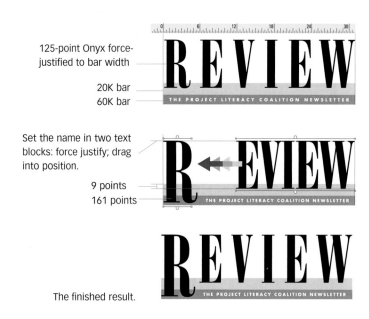

125-point Onyx force-justified to bar width

20K bar
60K bar

Set the name in two text blocks: force justify; drag into position.

9 points
161 points

The finished result.

The back page

Flow the text from the top margin (to align it with the front-page nameplate). When adding photos and quotes, make use of the six-column grid for precise alignment.

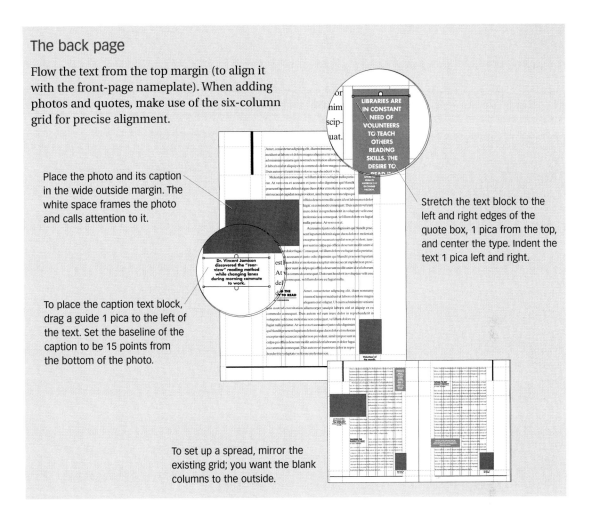

Place the photo and its caption in the wide outside margin. The white space frames the photo and calls attention to it.

To place the caption text block, drag a guide 1 pica to the left of the text. Set the baseline of the caption to be 15 points from the bottom of the photo.

Dr. Vincent Jamison discovered the "rear-view" reading method while changing lanes during morning commute to work.

LIBRARIES ARE IN CONSTANT NEED OF VOLUNTEERS TO TEACH OTHERS READING SKILLS, THE DESIRE TO READ "

Stretch the text block to the left and right edges of the quote box, 1 pica from the top, and center the type. Indent the text 1 pica left and right.

To set up a spread, mirror the existing grid; you want the blank columns to the outside.

To add a photograph above the headline

Place the photo across the two columns. Apply text wrap: Left, 1p0; Right, 1p0; Top, 0p3; Bottom, 4p6. Adjust the headline/byline spacing as shown. If it crowds the text, add space between the byline and text by adjusting the wrap tolerance.

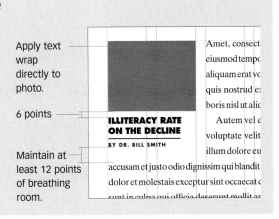

Apply text wrap directly to photo.

6 points

Maintain at least 12 points of breathing room.

ILLITERACY RATE ON THE DECLINE
BY DR. BILL SMITH

Amet, consect eiusmod tempo aliquam erat vo quis nostrud e: boris nisl ut alic
Autem vel e voluptate velit illum dolore eu accusam et justo odio dignissim qui blandit dolor et molestais exceptur sint occaecat c sunt in culpa qui officia deserunt mollit ar

A cross between paperback and magazine, this low-key, text-rich format is ideally suited for long, thoughtful articles—and it's easy to lay out.

This digest-size newsletter is for *readers*

Three of the most popular five magazines in America, *Reader's Digest, TV Guide*, and *National Geographic*, share an interesting physical trait: All three are smaller than regular magazines. Each is approximately digest size.

Paperback books are even more popular—and their pages are smaller still.

Is there something special about a small page? Sure! It's eminently portable.

A small page confines the reader's attention naturally. Its design, therefore, can be as quiet as a library. This makes it ideal for *education* or *business* topics. The designer is free to work on the words.

Upline calls itself a newsletter but is less *news* than instructional and motivational articles, the kind you'd find in seminars and schools. It's a perfect candidate for a digest: Its smooth, beautifully set stories are just right for putting up your feet for a good read.

Let's take it apart to see how it was done.

Great for short runs and small budgets, a digest can be published right in your office. Print two pages on each side of a letter-size sheet, then stack, fold and staple the results. Be aware that pages must be laid out in a different sequence than how you read them—in *printer spreads*. For example, in a 12-pager, page 1 abuts page 12, page 2 abuts page 11, and so on. The odd-numbered pages are always on the right. Lay out your pages normally if your layout program offers the option to build printer spreads or a booklet. Otherwise, fold yourself a paper dummy, number its pages, and figure the juxtaposition of pages from that.

Depth and variety in B&W

Look at what you can do in black and white! Synopsis-style contents makes the most of page 1, then tints of black add visual depth. The background should be your middle value (here 30 percent black), against which light and dark tints will have the greatest effect. Small type should have the highest contrast; note here the headlines are boldface white while the text is lightface black. Large type can be much more subtle; note shading of the nameplate (50 and 10 percent black). If your final output will be from a low-res printer, your background should remain white (below left).

The scholarly look

As easy to read as a book, this format imparts to its subject a sense of scholarship and authority that is difficult and often impossible to attain on showier pages. Set all in one type family (two if you want), its handsome typography provides visual variety without distractions.

The design has three key layouts: an article spread for feature stories, a news spread for briefs, and the table of contents, which this design carries on page 1.

As you work with it, you'll find that small type and pictures seem bigger than they do on normal pages, just like fish look bigger in a small bowl. That's a bonus of a digest: You can comfortably stuff (and read) more per inch than you otherwise could.

Page 1

Article spread

This digest-size newsletter is for *readers*   **7**

Wide margins impart a big-page look

The one-column grid is designed to accommodate a variety of features, some aesthetic, others for production efficiency. Its wide outer margins impart an expansive, big-page look—valuable in such a small space—and make room to extend pictures and callouts, which will provide visual relief from the gray columns. The narrower columns are made from ruler guides or text boxes, not column guides, so text will flow freely across them. In the few cases where the narrow columns are needed, just drag your text into position. Two middle horizontal guides mark the locations from which various texts will "hang."

Page specs

The specs for this page are: 33 × 51 picas, facing pages. The inside margin (in picas) is 3p; outside, 7p; top, 5p; and bottom, 5p. Zero rulers at top center. On the master pages or template, place vertical ruler guides at 29.5, 15.25 and 13.75 picas, both sides of center. Place the horizontal ruler guides at 2, 7 and 47.5 picas. **Note:** The cover has backward margins. Build it to fit a left-hand page, then make it page 1.

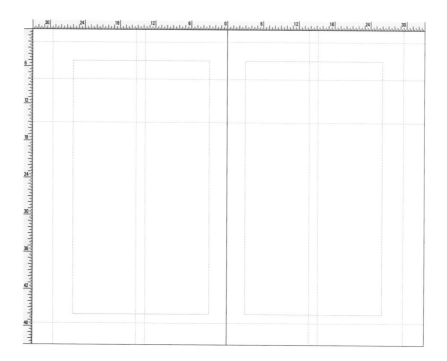

Typestyle sets the stage

Your choice of typestyle is the easiest place to establish your digest's visual character. For an authentic book look, use just a single typeface and its italic, with no bold at all (to also look *scholarly*, select an older typeface, such as Caslon). More flexible is a big type family, which includes bold and extra bold characters; typical is Century Condensed. Its contrasts give you many tones of voice, which you'll find helpful if you have a lot of subheads and miscellaneous items. For more difference, add a

display face (Poplar is used here) for headlines, drop caps and callouts. In every case, we recommend a light, serif typeface for text, to which readers are most accustomed.

Start at the top

The template is designed on a highly convenient 12-point grid and demonstrated by a single type family; the sizes given here are specific to this design. Your type sizes will have to be adjusted for the face(s) you choose.

All stories start at the top of a page with a kicker, headline, deckhead and a very large

initial drop cap. Note that the gray kicker box touches the edge; this will be truncated by a laser printer, in which case the box can be traded for an underline. Note, too, the first few words of text are set in small caps; this is one of those sophisticated details that requires individual attention and can be skipped if time is tight.

Set first few words in small caps

DOLLA **DOLLARS & SENSE** / Mar

When is a loss not a loss?

The 3-out-of-5-year "hobby rule" and "paper losses"

W HENEVE R BUSINESS EXPENSES exceed business income, a net loss is created. Depending upon the nature of the expenditures into legitimate writeoffs—see personal/Unique About an MLM Tax Return?" March "What's loss may not be a monetary loss but rather a 93), ti egative net income is not the goal of any profit-paper loss."Of course ted busin

Align drop cap with sixth text baseline

Kicker
Font: Century Light Condensed, 11/11

Department name: All caps, white

Byline: U&lc, black. Type insets 4 pts from edges of K50 bar

Headline
Font: Century Light Condensed 33/36, align left

Deckhead
Font: Century Light Condensed 15/18, align left

Text
Font: Century Light Condensed 10/12, justify

Drop cap
Font: Century Light Condensed 120/120, color K60

How to break up the page without artwork

If text is placidly flowing water, drop caps and large-type callouts are rocks in the riverbed— they create eddies and swirls that give the page a natural, visual appeal. Callouts go to the outside. Choose your text carefully: Callouts are read first and create a frame of reference for the entire spread. (A wise editor can put this to good use.) And stick to one drop cap per page. More than two on a spread, and your reader will try to figure out what they spell.

2nd page plain

2nd page with breaks

Three ways to start a new topic…

ore et dolore magna aliquam
quis nostrud exercitation ulla
ea commodo consequat.

Note that having a gross inco
You can literally have no incor
show no (zero) gross income
audit are high. Likewise, if yo
creases in the gross each yea
autem veleum irure dolor in r
vel illum dolore eu fugiat null

ore et dolore magna aliquam
quis nostrud exercitation ulla
ea commodo consequat.

YOU HAVE TO WANT TO C
not a requirement for profit m
still claim expenses! However,
than one year, your chances fo
gross income, with small incre
tive may be suspect. Duis aut
voluptate velit consequat vel

labore et dolore magna aliqua
mi quis nostrud exercitation
ex ea commodo consequat.

OTE THAT HAVING a
motive! You can l
penses! However,
than one year, yo
you show little gr
each year, your profit motive

Insert a line space…
One empty line is the shortest kind of pause other than a paragraph indent. The new line is not indented (no need for both kinds at once). This break can occur anywhere on the page, but it's most effective near the middle.

OR use a bold phrase…
A phrase in bold will draw the eye more sharply. After a line break, simply set the first few words of the next sentence in bold type. Be sure to be consistent: Caps, if used once, should be used every time.

AND try a drop cap
A drop cap creates by far the biggest ripple in the text. Unlike the lead cap, secondary caps like this are five, not six lines deep. Note, too, the gray color (60 percent black). Size and color serve to tone down the effect.

Callouts draw the reader in

A callout aligns with a center ruler guide and extends into the outside margin. Note text flows uniformly around; any extra space goes underneath the callout. Best locations (below) are top, bottom and at 15 pica.

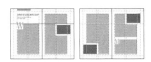

Space: 1p6

Minimum 1p6 space

Callout
Font: Century Light Condensed 16/18, align left

Filler stories are tiny vacations

All work and no play makes even bright readers wish they were elsewhere. A smart editor will relieve the weight of feature articles with a variety of short, preferably light, ones. The perfect place for these is the leftover spaces at the end of long articles. Fill with reports, quotations, cartoons, whatever. It's smart to build a library of material of various lengths.

News filler

Gray background box extends from outer ruler guide 1 pica past the inside margin. The head is set 18/18 and is aligned left. Lead paragraph is set in italics 10/12, justified and the two-column text is one point size smaller, 8/12, and is justified.

Quotation filler

Capitalize and center the head, italicize the body, 10/12, justified, and set the attribution in small caps, tabbed right or aligned right. Rule above quote is 2 points. To be ideal, the space between the items would stay consistent, but it can be adjusted to fit.

Two columns for flexibility

News pages are set in two columns divided by a vertical rule, which differentiates them clearly from feature articles. Type is designed in several "levels" to accommodate different kinds of articles and tones of voice. This enables the editor to tune each story to the exact volume and pitch it warrants. It also avoids the visual choppiness often found on news pages. For variety, news pages make full use of the template's narrow outer margins.

News

Three new 2-day seminars

Boston, Dec. 9–10, 1999
Management and accounting for the home-based business
Lorem ipsum dolor sit amet, consectetur adipscing elit, diam nonnumy eius mod tempor incidunt ut labore et dolore magna aliquam erat volu pat. Ut enim minimim veniami quis nost rud exer citation ullam corper susci pit lab oris nisl aliquip ex conse quat. Duis au tem vel eum irure dolor in rep rehende rit in voluptate vel it esse taie son con sequat, vel illum dolore eu fug iat nulla pari atur. At vero eos et accus am et justo odio dignissim qui blandit.

Miami, Feb. 4–6, 1999
How to handle out-of-state sales for the home-based business
Lorem ipsum dolor sit amet, consec-lupatum delenit aigue duos dolor et exceptur sint occaecat cupi dat non provi dent, simil tempor sunt in. Culpa qui officia deserunt mollit an imid laborum fugai. Et harumd dere ud facilis et expe

Upline™ subscriptions
MULS-01 Annual subscription $69
MULS-02 Two-year subscription $120
MULS-03 Foreign (surface) $79
MULS-05 Foreign (airmail) $93
MULS-07 Sample issue $6
MULS-08 Lifetime subscription $1000
Prices include postage and handling

Please direct all inquiries and orders to: Upline, 310 E. Main St. #150, Charlottesville, VA 22901—or phone our 24-hour voice mail: 1-800-800-6349

dit distinct. Liber a tempor. Cam soluta nobis eligend optio comque nihil quod a impedit anim id quod maxim plac eat facer possim omnis voluptas assumen da est, omnis dolor repellend. Tempor em eutem quinsud aur office debit aut tum rerum necessit saepe eveniet rep udiand sint noneste recusand. Itaque ear ud rerum tentur sapiente delectus.

Dallas, June 16–17, 1999
How to gauge the market and price your product accordingly
Lorem ipsum dolor sit amet, consec. Cam soluta nobis eligend optio comque nihil quod a impedit anim id. Lorem ip sum dolor sit amet, consectetur adip scing elit, diam nonnumy ei us mod tempor incidunt ut labore et dolore ma gna aliquam erat volupat. Ut enim min imim veniami quis nost rud exercita tion ullam corper susci pit laboris nisl aliquip ex consequat. Duis autem vel eum irure dolor in reprehenderit in vol uptate velit esse taie son con sequat, vel illum dolore eu fugiat nulla paria-tur. At vero eos et accus am et justo odio dignissim qui blandit praesent lu patum delenit aigue duos dolor et ex ceptur sint occaecat cupi dat non pro vident, simil tempor sunt in culpa qui offi cia des erunt mollit an imid est la-bor um et dolor fugai. Et harumd dere ud facilis at vero eoset accus am et justo odio. Ut enim min imim veniami.

President Smith to appear with Jay Leno

Lorem ipsum do-lor sit amet, con-sectetur adipscing elitam, diam non-numy esmod tem-por incidun labore dolore mag na ali-quam erat. Ut eni ad minimim veniami quis nostrud ex-ercitation ullamcorper suscipit labor-is nisl ut aliquip ex ea commodo con-sequat. Duis autem vel eum irure do-lor in reprehenderit in voluptate velit esse molestaie son consequat, vel il-lum dolore fugiat nulla pariatur. At vero eos et accusam et justo odio dig-nissim qui blandit praesent lupatum delenit aigue duos dolor et molestais exceptur sint occaecat cupidat non provident, simil tempor sunt in culpa qui officia deserunt mollit anim id est laborum et dolor fugai.

Raul Edwards tops $40,000 in one month

Et harumd dereud facilis est er expe-dit distinct. Nam liber a tempor com soluta nobis eligend optio comque ni-hil quod a impedit anim id quod maxim placeat facer possim omnis es volup-tas assumenda est, omnis dolor repel-lend. Temporem eutem quinsud et aur office debit aut tum rerum necessit atib saepe eveniet ut er repudiand sint et molestia non este recusand. Itaque earud rerum hic tentury sapiente de-lectus au aut prefer endis dolorib as-

periore repellat. Hanc ego com tene sentniam, quid est cur verear ne ad eam non possing accommodare nost ros quos tu paulo ante com memorite it tum etia ergat. Nos amice et nebe-vol, olestias access potest fier ad au-gendas com conscient to factor tum toen legum odioque civiuda. Et tamen in busdad ne que pecun modut est neque nonor imper ned libiding gen epular religuard on cupiditat, quas null umdnat. Improb pary minuiti potius inflammad ut coercend magist and et dodecendense videantur, invitat igtur vera ratio bene santos ad iustitiami aequitated fidem. Neque hominy infant aut inuiste fact est cond que neg fac-ile efficerd possit duo conteud notiner si effecerit, et opes vel forunag veling en liberalitat magis em conveniunt, dabut tutungbene volent sib conciliant et, al is adtissim est ad quiet. Endium caritat praesert com omning null siy caus peccand quaerer en imigent cu-pidat a natura proficis facile explent sine julla inura autend unanc sunt isti. Et harumd dereud facilis est er expe-dit distinct. Nam liber a tempor com soluta nobis eligend optio com que nihail quod an impedit canimo pida quodi maxim plaiceat facer possim omnis es voluptas assumenda est, omnis dolor repellend.

Temporem eutem quinsud et aur of-fice debit aut tum rerum necessit atib saepe eveniet ut er repudiand.

Four head levels

1 Flags the section. Black box draws the eye to very light type.
   Century Light Condensed 48/48, align left

2 An umbrella covering separate but closely related articles.
   Century Light Condensed 24/24, align left

3 Minor heads related directly to umbrella.
   Century Ultra Condensed 9/12, align left

4 For news stories that stand alone. One, two or three lines deep.
   Century Light Condensed, 15/15, align left

Subheads have an important voice

No opportunity for good communication is more often overlooked than the simple sub-head. While the job of a news headline is to report impersonally, a subhead can speak quite naturally. It can be used to expand a headline's meaning, as it does here, but it's also the best place to address your readers in your every-day voice.

Century Light Condensed Italic 9/12, align left. Indent 1p0.

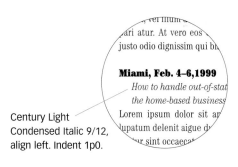

Half-column photos

As with drop caps and callouts, think of photos as rocks in a riverbed and always make sure your type can flow around them; don't create a dam. Two types are illustrated here: rectangular and silhouette. Rectangular photos should all be the same width; a half-column is ideal. Silhouettes can be bigger; they are more inter-esting and will be perceived as more important. Near the silhouette is an excellent place for an important caption, like an announcement, because everyone will read it.

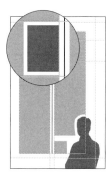

Adjust news heads for fit

Three goals here: You need the flexibility of one-, two-, and three-line headlines, which don't all land on the grid; you want your text to align horizontally across columns, and you want the empty spaces to look even. This can all be done by adjusting *Spacing before.*

News head: Century Light Condensed 15/15, align left, set all Spacing after to 0p6

Text aligns
across columns

> modut cae neque nona imper nica nb
> tur adipscing elitamo, diam nonnumy
> esmod tempor incidun labore dolore
> mag na aliquam erat.
>
> ## Raul Edwards tops out!
>
> Et harumd dereud facilis est er expe-
> dit distinct. Nam liber a tempor com
> soluta nobis eligend optio comque ni-
> hil quod a impedit anim id quod maxim
> placeat facer possim omnis.
>
> ## Raul Edwards tops $40,000 in September
>
> Et harumd dereud facilis est er expe-
> dit distinct. Nam liber a tempor com
> soluta nobis eligend optio comque ni-
> hil quod a impedit anim id quod maxim
> placeat facer possim omnis.
>
> ## Salesman of the month Raul Edwards tops $40,000 in September
>
> Et harumd dereud facilis est er expe-
> dit distinct. Nam liber a tempor com
> soluta nobis eligend optio comque ni-

> amice. et
> test fier ad
> factor tum
> da. Et tam
> modut est
> iding gen
> tat, quas
> minuiti po
> magist and
> invitat igtu
> iustitiami a
> miny infan
> que neg fa
> teud notin
> forunag ve
> conveniunt
> sib concilia
> com memo
> amice et r
> test fier ad
> factor tum
> da. Et tam
> modut est
> iding gen
> tat, quas
> minuiti po
> magist and
> invitat igtu
> iustitiami a
> miny infan
> que neg fa

1-line head: Space once after the last paragraph, then add 0p3 Spacing before to the head.

2-line head: Space twice after the last paragraph, then set the head.

3-line head: Space once after the last paragraph, then add 0p9 Spacing before to the head.

7 | Back pages

Leave room for the mailing label

A digest is almost always stapled but rarely folded and therefore mails flat. A half-page space for the label is typical, but you can get away with less. Check with the post office before finalizing your design. Whatever you choose, be consistent from issue to issue. Note that a small nameplate is part of the return address.

> molestais exceptur sint occaecat cupidat non provident, simil tempor sunt
> in culpa qui officia deserunt mollit anim id est laborum et dolor fugai. Et
> harumd dereud facilis est er expedit distinct. nam liber a tempor cum
> soluta nobis eligend optio comque nihil quod a impedit anim id quod maxim
> placeat facer possim omnis es voluptat assumenda est, omnis dolor repel-
> lend. Temporem eutem quinsud et aur office debit aut tum rerum neces-
> sit atih saepe eveniet ut er repudiand sint et molestia non este recusand.
> Itaque earud rerum hic tentury sapiente delectus au aut pefer endis do-
> lorib asperiore repellat. Hane ego cum tene sentniam, quid est cur verear
> ne ad eam non possing accommodare nost ros quos tu paulo ante cum
> memorie it tum etia ergat. Nos amice et nebevol, olestias access potest
> fier ad augendas cum conscient to factor tum toen legum odioque civiu-
> da. Et tamen in busdad ne que pecun modut est neque nonor imper ned
> libiding gen epular religuard on cupiditat, quas nulla praid im umdnat.
> Improb pary minuiti potius inflammad ut coercend magist and et dode-
> cendese videautur, invitat igtur vera ratio bene santos ad iustitiami aequi-
> tated fidem. Neque hominy infant aut inuiste fact est cond que negi facile
> efficerd possit duo conteud notiner si effecerit, et opes vel forunag veling
> en libaralitat magis em convenunt, dabut tutunghene suntir sib concili-
> iant et, al is adtiasim est ad quiet. Endium caritat praesert cum omning.
>
> ## Upline
>
> 310 East Main Street
> Suite 150
> Charlottesville VA 22902
>
> US Second Class
> Postage Paid

How to name your newsletter

Naming a newsletter can be tough: Titles can sound corny, dull, trite or all three. And the best design in the world can't compensate for a dumb name or a mediocre idea. Tricks and easy turns-of-phrase usually have no regard what really must be done: communication.

Here are several suggestions: One, in working out a name, whether it is for a newsletter or a product or a whole business, the best advice is to do it alone. You are the only one who cares. Usually, committees don't come up with good names. (If you are already on a committee, assign the job to the person who has the strongest feelings about it.) Similarly, don't poll office colleagues or friends; as much as they may try, they can't be objective.

Your feedback should, and can, come from one source only, your potential readers. This is the key. No matter how much you—or the boss—like the name, if readers yawn, no design can save it.

To name your newsletter, think *outside-in*. That is, think like a reader. You will realize that a reader responds only when his or her personal interests, opinions and preferences are clearly addressed.

For example, if your name is George, you may be personally flattered by *The George Report*, but how does a reader see it? To get the idea, visualize your name on someone else's product. Then, you can be more objective. *The Doe Report* is less interesting, isn't it?

Corny names are often the result of disrespect for the product or the reader. Label-type names can be dull because they usually give the reader no point of entry. For example, *Update* is a common but closed name. To see this, compare *Informer, Spy, Tattler* and *Juice*. They may not be appropriate for your publication, but each is open-ended; that is, each engages the reader—in these cases, by hinting at inside information.

Open your thesaurus. Find words with meanings common to everyone. Look for picture words: *Gibraltar*, for example, is much better than *solid* or *trustworthy. Olympus* is richer than *powerful*.

If your name or reputation is very well known, you should use it in your publication name.

Most important, persist. Your name is extremely valuable, and it is worth every minute it takes to find the right one.

Consistency and variation can work together.

Clean, asymmetrical layout leads the eye

The creator of this newsletter wanted an asymmetrical look for his newsletter, a departure from the run-of-the-mill, three-column, desktop-published page. He would use most of his page for text, and the empty column, set to the inside, would be reserved for pictures, captions, callouts and miscellaneous information.

His idea was good; the results were disappointing—yet the *makeover*, he said, was the look he'd had in mind.

But had he come close? Judge for yourself.

Type *faux pas*

Unlike other graphics, a font speaks English, so its shape, size and position on the page exert covert and inescapable influence on the mind of the reader.

The reader will respond to a word set in dense bold type differently than to the same word set in a light face, or say, a condensed face. *Each variation makes a unique statement.* Here, *The Weigand Report* nameplate should send a unified message, yet it has been set in two fonts, four sizes, on four baselines in at least seven variations. So while the reader understands the English, the unspoken messages clash, contradict and weaken the page.

A cacophony of type styles, sizes, positions and other variations bewilder the eye, which searches for a focal point and finds none.

Here, type has been toned down, the page organized into four visual areas: banner, headline, text and contents. The eye can now move smoothly.

Edition number and **date** are set on opposite margins, newspaper-style. Result: attention is drawn to almost insignificant data.

Who is this man? The article is about the frenetic pace of computer development, but the designer probably saw the word *Race* and used clip art to picture that concept. This was a mistake. A useful illustration would have supported the article with additional information; for example, a timeline that showed the overwhelming pace of innovation.

A picture used as a space filler may get by the boss, but its value to the reader is zero.

Columns of justified text define their own space; **column rules** are unnecessary.

PAGE 1 AFTER

The WEIGAND Report

The Working Newsletter for Desktop Publishers

Issue Number 4   January 1990

Outlook for the 1990's—The Race for New Standards!

The new decade promises exciting advances in desktop computing, with the possibility of several "breakthrough" products setting new standards. Companies that successfully develop and implement new standards stand to reap huge financial rewards, so the race for technological leadership is intense. Competition among the giants rages fiercely at times (sometimes at the expense of the consumer), and the game often is played under no-holds-barred rules.

In the font arena, for example, Apple recently severed ties with long-time ally Adobe and announced Royal, a new outline-font scheme they hope will replace Adobe's PostScript standard. Apple, in fact, may produce a worthwhile and competitive product, but they run the risk of alienating a large segment of their installed customer base, those whom they encouraged earlier to invest extensively in expensive PostScript technology.

Adobe, for their part, is battling back with innovative products like ATM (Adobe Type Manager), and a promise to unveil their proprietary font-hinting routines to third-party vendors. Microsoft has joined with Apple, but Big Blue has yet to make a final commitment. IBM's choice of a font technology could deter-

mine the overall outcome of the standards battle because of the enormous buying power of legions of loyal PC users under their dominion.

As we roll into the 1990's, various competing platforms are beginning to look alike. For example, entrenched IBM advocates soon will be upgrading to Windows 3.0, a revision that brings to PCs many of the most envied graphical-interface niceties of the Macintosh (the much heralded OS-2, on the other hand, failing to gain wide acceptance, soon may die an unsung death). Gaining momentum in the background is Display PostScript, a dark horse that, because of NeXT, still has a shot at the title. If this apparent convergence toward a common graphical interface continues, your buying choices soon may be based on the availability and performance of task-specific software instead of the hardware on which it must run.

The new decade also will see continued upheaval in the fast-changing peripherals market. CD-ROM vendors are silently praying CD-ROM sales pick up before prices of read-write optical disks decline to more inviting levels. Both kinds of drives, however, may become obsolete quickly if an alternate technology, like the laser card (a high-density,

compact credit-card-size storage medium), becomes popular. Before long, futuristic storage devices still on today's drawing boards could make today's hard disks resemble prehistoric artifacts.

Over the next few years you'll also see artificial intelligence (AI) tools finally make their way into popular page-makeup programs. Groupware applications, especially, will benefit as AI tools help to standardize final document output, regardless of how complex the production cycle or how many individuals are involved in the editing process. By the end of the decade, almost every publishing program of note will incorporate some degree of AI assistance.

This is but a tiny preview of what's yet to come. As new standards emerge, many old ones will continue to hold sway, especially where users have a substantial investment in the current technology. As a working desktop publisher, you'll be faced with an ever-increasing array of difficult and often conflicting choices from vendors who may not fully appreciate your needs. Fortunately, though, the buying decisions you make will determine which standards survive, and which get discarded. Choose wisely, and we'll all benefit. —*CJW*

IN THIS ISSUE:

The **WEIGAND** Report 1

The Weigand Report

THE WORKING NEWSLETTER FOR DESKTOP PUBLISHERS

Outlook for the 1990s:
The Race for New Standards

THE NEW DECADE promises exciting advances in desktop computing, with the possibility of several breakthrough products setting new standards. Companies that successfully develop and implement new standards stand to reap huge financial rewards, so the race for leadership is intense. Competition among the giants rages fiercely (sometimes at the expense of the consumer), and the game often is played under no-holds-barred rules.

In the font arena, Apple recently severed ties with long-time ally Adobe and announced Royal, a new outline-font scheme they hope will replace Adobe's PostScript standard. Apple may produce a worthwhile and competitive product, but they risk alienating a large part of their installed customer base, those whom they encouraged earlier to invest extensively in expensive PostScript technology.

Adobe, for their part, is battling back with innovative products like Adobe Type Manager and a promise to unveil their font-hinting routines to third-party vendors. Microsoft has joined Apple, but Big Blue has yet to make a committment. IBM's choice of a font technology could determine the outcome of the standards battle because of the huge buying power of loyal PC users under their dominion.

As we roll into the 1990s, various competing platforms are beginning to look alike. For example,

IBM advocates soon will be upgrading to Windows 3.0, a revision that brings to PCs many of the most envied graphical-interface niceties of the Macintosh (the much heralded OS-2, on the other hand, failing to gain wide acceptance, may die an unsung death). Gaining momentum in the background is Display PostScript, a dark horse that, because of NeXT, still has a shot at the title. If this convergence toward a common graphical interface continues, your buying choices soon may be based on the availability and performance of task-specific software instead of the hardware on which it must run.

The new decade also will see upheaval in the fast-changing peripherals market. CD-ROM vendors are praying CD-ROM sales pick up before prices of read-write optical disks decline to more inviting levels. Both kinds of drives, however, may become obsolete quickly if an alternate technology, like the laser card (a high-density, compact credit-card-size storage medium), becomes popular. Before long, futuristic storage devices still on today's drawing boards could make today's hard disks resemble prehistoric artifacts.

Over the next few years you'll also see artificial intelligence (AI) tools finally make their way into page-makeup programs. Groupware applications, especially, will benefit as AI tools help to standardize final document output, regardless of how complex the production cycle or how many individuals are involved in the editing process. By the end of the decade, almost every publishing program of note will incorporate some degree of AI assistance.

As new standards emerge, many old ones will continue to hold sway, especially where users have a substantial investment in the current technology. As a desktop publisher, you'll be faced with an increasing array of difficult and often conflicting choices from vendors who may not fully appreciate your needs. Fortunately, the buying decisions you make will determine which standards survive, and which get discarded.—CJW

The **Weigand** Report
ISSUE NUMBER 4 / JANUARY 1990

Headline is set in italics, which are normally used to show motion or emphasis. That's unnecessary—heck, it's already the headline. Similarly, the big initial *O* is unnecessary.

Four columns of materials is too much for three columns. The text must be unnecessarily small and the columns very narrow, and there is no room to maneuver. In this newsletter, page 2 holds notable material—the editorial—yet its title, News & Views, must be shoe-horned into a space so tight that it appears insignificant. The makeover uses the extra space to let the title and headline flourish.

The bulk of its contents in three columns, the page is heavily unbalanced to the left and down, which draws subliminal attention to the page itself and disrupts the editorial message.

Although the headline would fit on one line, it looks better in two. Concentrated, the eye remains focused above the article it is about to read.

The editor's name and the page title were handled like on a book cover: identical type, same size, equal billing. Reversing the sequence would shift the emphasis ever so subtly.

New page **folio** matches the text and imparts its modest information quietly. Unimportant data like this should not stand out.

Issue Number 4 **The Working Newsletter for Desktop Publishers** *January 1990*

News & Views by C. J. Weigand

News & Views analyzes what's happening in the industry to bring you pertinent, up-to-date news and commentary. We identify trends that may impact your business and recommend actions for you to stay competitive. We also test and review software and hardware products to help you make effective buying decisions. We call things as we see them, and we try to see them from your point of view, that of the working desktop publisher.

Computer Viruses—Threat for a New Decade

Nothing is more devastating than to be hit with a malicious viral attack. Viruses are insidious little rascals with a well-deserved reputation for bringing production work to a sudden and total halt. If you don't set up an impenetrable defense well in advance, you can expect someday to get ransacked. No one is immune.

The computer viral threat looms large on the horizon for the 1990s. As we enter the new decade, perpetrators are actively waging new assaults on innocent and unsuspecting computer users. And the number of viruses in circulation is escalating. While no one yet fully understands what goes on in the minds of individuals who set out to do this kind of criminal mischief, one thing is certain—there are enough jerks out there that it's going to get worse before it gets better.

Viruses are computer codes that covertly attach to programs. Unpredictable results occur once a virus is unleashed. Applications may function unreliably or simply freeze; routine tasks may take longer to execute; computers may crash often; startup disks may fail to boot; files may explode in size and become inaccessible; documents may not print properly; in short, your entire system may become erratic or unusable.

Methods of viral transmission vary, but sharing or downloading public domain or pirated software is the surest way to get infected. If you download a contaminated file from a BBS or across a network, you can easily infect your hard disk. A virus also can remain hidden in a compressed file (*Stuffit* is a popular file compression utility) undetectable (and impotent) until the file is unstuffed. After the virus is released, it becomes infectious.

Some viruses lie dormant for a long time (determined in advance by the programmer), only to activate days, weeks, or even months after initial exposure. Keep in mind that the goal of every virus is go unnoticed while replicating until the maximum amount of spread has occurred.

Make no mistake about it. It's all-out war, and you're the target. Even well-intentioned viruses, like the famous "World Peace" message of a couple years ago, can do extensive damage. After all, it's tough enough to write legitimate code without also trying to make viruses "bug free."

What can you do? Don't trust any external contact with your computer system. Test everything before using it. And that includes commercial software, which may arrive in its shrink-wrapped box already infected (it's happened on more than one occasion). Use a good viral-prevention software to unmask invaders and prevent infection.

After you initially verify that your system is clean, install a viral-prevention software and keep it active at all times. Make multiple backups of new programs, and continually backup all your work files. Always keep the write-protect tabs on master disks locked. And, most importantly, once you establish an effective system of safeguards, absolutely never bypass it. The one time you ignore your defenses could be the one time you get clobbered.

Proper use of antiviral software can completely eliminate the risk of casual infection.

Combating Viruses

Destructive computer viruses continue to appear at an alarming rate. The latest scourge is a totally new kind of virus that attacks the invisible Desktop file on your System disk and installs a WDEF resource. Infection may be accompanied by a series of frequent and unpredictable system crashes. Unfortunately, most existing programs that claim to automatically detect new viral strains were unable to recognize this new WDEF virus when it first appeared (the single exception was Anti-Virus Kit from 1st Aid Software). Consequently, the WDEF virus spread quickly throughout the Macintosh community. This reinforces our argument — *Continued on page 4*

2 **The WEIGAND Report**

NEWS&VIEWS
C.J.WEIGAND

Computer Viruses: Threat for a New Decade

News & Views analyzes what's happening in the industry to bring you pertinent, up-to-date news and commentary. We identify trends that may impact your business and recommend actions for you to stay competitive. We also test and review software and hardware products to help you make effective buying decisions. We call things as we see them, and we try to see them from your point of view, that of the working desktop publisher.

NOTHING IS MORE DEVASTATING than to be hit with a malicious viral attack. Viruses are insidious little rascals with a well-deserved reputation for bringing production work to a sudden and total halt. If you don't set up an impenetrable defense well in advance, you can expect someday to get ransacked. No one is immune.

The computer viral threat looms large on the horizon for the 1990s. As we enter the new decade, perpetrators are actively waging new assaults on innocent and unsuspecting computer users. And the number of viruses in circulation is escalating. While no one yet fully understands what goes on in the minds of individuals who set out to do this kind of criminal mischief, one thing is certain—there are enough jerks out there that it's going to get worse before it gets better.

Viruses are computer codes that covertly attach to programs. Unpredictable results occur once a virus is unleashed. Applications may function unreliably or simply freeze; routine tasks may take longer to execute; computers may crash often; startup disks may fail to boot ; files may explode in size and become inaccessible; documents may not print properly; in short, your entire system may become erratic or unusable.

Methods of viral transmission vary, but sharing or downloading public domain or pirated software is the surest way to get infected. If you download a contaminated file from a BBS or across a network, you can easily infect your hard disk. A virus also can remain hidden in a compressed file (*Stuffit* is a popular file compression utility) undetectable (and impotent) until the file is unstuffed. After the virus is released, it becomes infectious.

Some viruses lie dormant for a long time (determined in advance by the programmer), only to activate days, weeks, or even months after initial exposure. Keep in mind that the goal of every virus is go unnoticed while replicating until the maximum amount of spread has occurred.

Make no mistake about it. It's all-out war, and you're the target. Even well-intentioned viruses, like the famous "World Peace" message of a couple years ago, can do extensive damage. After all, it's tough enough to write legitimate code without also trying to make viruses "bug free."

What can you do? Don't trust any external contact with your computer system. Test everything before using it. And that includes commercial software, which may arrive in its shrink-wrapped box already infected (it's happened on more than one occasion). Use a good viral-prevention software to unmask invaders and prevent infection.

After you initially verify that your system is clean, install a viral-prevention software and keep it active at all times. Make multiple backups of new programs, and continually backup all your work files. Always keep the write-protect tabs on master disks locked. And, most importantly, once you establish an effective system of safeguards, never bypass it. The one time you ignore your defenses could be the one time you get clobbered.

Combating Viruses

Destructive computer viruses continue to appear at an alarming rate. The latest scourge is a totally new kind of virus that attacks the invisible continued on page 4

2   The Weigand Report / January 1990

1   Stencil a nameplate

The stencil effect on our sample newsletter's nameplate is a cinch to do and can be applied to an endless variety of fonts. Here's how:

Set a word
In any font; bold is usually best. We used Helvetica Inserat.

Kern tightly
Most large type looks more authoritative tightly set.

Rule lines
Experiment with placement (dark lines are easier to position). Print often to proof.

Color lines
Match background; here it's just white.

2   New two-column page has seven columns

A surprising, seven-column grid underlies the makeover. The right six columns hold the text in two columns; the left column is used for everything else. Anything placed in the empty column should "flirt" with its adjacent text; the interaction, which results, gives the pages its balance and visual interest. Try it but be patient. Refer to the model in step 3 to stay simple.

The seven-column format is energetic, extremely flexible and a lot of fun to work with—it forms a foundation suitable for literally thousands of layouts in nearly any typeface. This makeover uses two: Helvetica Inserat (a bold sans serif very similar to Helvetica Black Condensed used at 9/12 for subheads and 30/30 for headlines) and Janson Roman, a wonderfully readable text font similar to old-style Garamond (10/12 for text and 78/78 for the large cap).

Page specs

Here are the measurements used for this model: letter-size page, portrait orientation; inside margin of 4p6; outside margin, 4p; top margin 5p; and bottom margin, 5p. There are seven columns, with 1 pica between each.

Font specs

Text: Janson Roman 10/12
Subheads: Helvetica Inserat 9/12
Headlines: Helvetica Inserat 30/30
Large cap: Janson Roman 78/78

Text, set on 12-point leading, aligns with 1-pica ruler increments, or multiples or divisibles of 1 pica.

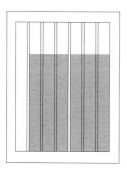

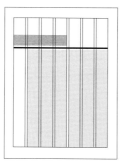

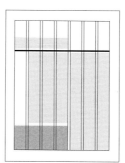

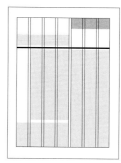

Text blocks each cross three columns, an excellent reading width.

Head and underline extend to left margin, easily balancing the page.

Element at lower left extends to left margin. Could extend further right.

Section head or graphic aligns with column 5 at top, maintains balance.

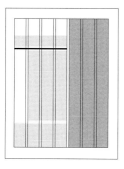

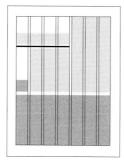

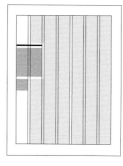

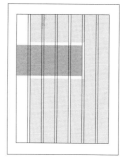

Section heading crosses four columns; text extends to top.

Large picture or sidebar crosses all columns; caption is above it.

Small picture or callout "flirts" with text, maintains balance and interest.

Oops. Avoid interrupting full column in middle of page; you'll make the reader jump!

What can you do with a few pieces of clip art and a tight schedule?
Lots! Just think *round.*

Easy! A simple, *do-able* look

Bananas was, at its outset, a delightful news-letter already. Created for a child-care referral service, its feel is *approachable* (a hard quality to capture), literate, easy to digest and alto-gether pleasant—qualities perfect for an audi-ence of nervous parents.

But *Bananas* could use a *look*. A visual style, even a simple one, is as important as a written style. It conveys a sense of who you are to the reader before he reads a word. Besides that, the newsletter is just one of many documents Bananas—the organization—publishes, and a look carefully applied to each of them will silently tell the reader they speak with the same voice. Such a look is like a signature; it can be

so valuable that big companies often spend millions of dollars to make sure this public "face" is the same no matter where it appears.

In *Bananas'* case, however, there is another issue to address: The newsletter is so simple that it can't be redesigned without complicating production, something its busy creator does not have time for. A signature style, therefore, must be simple, too. To achieve this, the make-over relies on the look of a single, distinct typeface—VAG Rounded—and round shapes. This technique—using squares, triangles, shades, whatever—works with many projects and a wide range of typefaces. Check out these examples.

A bouncy new name

Any program that can rotate text in small increments can build the wiggly headline. Set each character as a separate text block, then rotate the letters two or three degrees (no more than that) and move them around.

It's easy to go overboard with this kind of thing: You might be tempted to make the word *newsletter* bounce, too. Resist! Note how the bold underline mimics the style and weight of the name.

AFTER

Bananas

newsletter

April–May 1990 / Vol. XV, No. 4

Spring arrives along with a **San Francisco Foundation** grant to assist nonprofit centers in becoming "earthquake-ready." BANANAS will be contacting centers in the near future to make an appointment for a free check of common earthquake hazards which will include minor preparedness repairs such as securing water heaters and toy cabinets to the walls, etc. As part of this grant BANANAS will also be offering for sale, at a greatly reduced price, a unique combination radio/flashlight which does not use batteries. Child care programs wishing to purchase this invaluable device for future emergencies can come to BANANAS with a check for $20 (or send a check for $25 if you want us to mail it to you). Many thanks to the San Francisco Foundation for making this innovative project possible.

With spring comes Mother's Day, a holiday which started as a mother's plea for world peace. Again this year there will be a **Mother's Day Peace Walk** in Berkeley to commemorate and give strength to that sentiment. It's a lovely way to relax with your children on Mother's Day, be entertained and picnic in the park (bring a lunch; free Ben & Jerry ice cream provided). It's on **May 13 at** noon at Martin Luther King Park on MILK Jr. Way between Allston and Center. For more information, call 548-9165.

The census is in full swing. We urge everyone to be counted because the need for many services is projected based on these numbers. And if you work in child care there is a concerted effort to upgrade and recognize our profession by reporting our occupations uniformly: *Prekindergarten Teachers, Child Care Assistants, Family Child Care Providers, Child Care Workers/Private Household* (caregivers working in the child's home) and *Early Childhood Administrators* (directors or

Our thanks to the families who have contributed to the **Eula Hester Memorial Fund.** Eula was the warm, loving co-director (with her husband, Wesley) of Hester's Day Nursery for over 30 years. She died in November. We and many East Bay families miss her. Contributions will be used to provide training scholarships for child care workers.

One column is easy to pour, but shorter lines are easier on the eye

Even with pictures, the very long lines used below are a bit fatiguing, so the makeover uses two columns, each a more normal reading length. Type that's aligned left (rather than justified) and that has wider margins (4p6) lightens the look. Original Helvetica was set 10.5 points on 12.5 point leading. The new Century Expanded is set 10/12. Since Century Expanded is slightly smaller than Helvetica, the new text is airier and more relaxed.

BEFORE

News-in-a-box is special

Any article that's isolated like this will attract special attention. Tinting the border medium gray helps keep it from looking fence-like. (This is always a problem with boxes—those borders tend to clutter things. If output is to be at high resolution, avoid borders entirely and instead fill shapes with 10 or 20 percent gray.)

Note how the bunny sticks out of the box. This is an extremely effective cropping technique that works more often than not. Compare the bunny to the girl in the "before" version—see how she looks contained? Try this with other art; The results are quite satisfactory.

1 The basics of a look

If ever there was a typographic baby face, it is VAG Rounded, whose soft, rounded forms have a child-like touchability that is perfect for a child-care newsletter.

VAG Rounded makes me think *nursery*, of those Fisher-Price toys and Sesame Street—and it sets the theme for everything that follows. As you add features, think *round*: Initial capital letters are set into round-cornered boxes, bold bars have round ends…

…and even the contrasting serif face, Century Expanded, has been selected for its round feel. Note how the smooth curves of the serifs and dots on letters *l, r* and *g* (as well as others) help maintain the round look.

2 A signature style

Key to the makeover is the consistent style of VAG Rounded Black as an accent face. Note that page headings and headlines are set in VAG, but so are the words in the text, which would ordinarily be set in bold. It's more trouble to set type this way, but it preserves what is otherwise a very simple look.

BEFORE

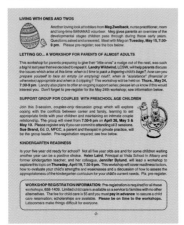

Sidebar type contrasts with text type
If sidebars, listings and other special articles (like the one on the first page of this article) are set in VAG Light—as they are here—they contrast with the text, and the eye immediately identifies the information as different from the rest.

AFTER

Bananas' Workshops

Living with ones and twos

Another loving look at toddlers from **Meg Zweiback**, nurse practitioner, mom and long-time BANANAS volunteer. Meg gives parents an overview of the developmental stages children pass through during these early years. Questions asked and answered. Meet with Meg on **Tuesday, May 15, 7:30–9:00 p.m.** Please register in advance; see below.

Letting go . . . A workshop for parents of almost adults

This workshop for parents preparing to give their "little ones" a nudge out of the nest is such a big hit last year that we decided to repeat it. **Landry Wildwind**, LCSW, will help parents discuss the issues which arise at this time: *When is it time to pack a lingering child's bags? How can you prepare yourself to face an empty (or emptying) nest? When is "assistance" (financial or otherwise) appropriate and when is it crippling?* This workshop will be held on **Thursday, May 24, 7:30– 9:00 p.m.** Landry also plans to offer an ongoing support series; please let us know if this would interest you. Don't forget to register in advance for the May 24th workshop; see information below.

Support groups for couples with preschool-age children

Join this 3-session, *couples-only* discussion group which will explore coping with the conflicts between career and family, learning to set appropriate limits with your children and maintaining an intimate couple relationship. The group will meet **7:30–9:00 p.m.** on **April 26, May 3** and **May 10**. Please register only if you can commit to attending all three sessions. **Sue Brand**, Ed.D, MFCC, a parent and therapist in private practice, will be the group leader. Advance registration required.

Kindergarten readiness

Is your five-year-old ready for school? Not all five-year-olds are and for some children waiting another year can be a positive choice. **Helen Laird**, Principal at Vista School in Albany and former kindergarten teacher, and her colleague **Jennifer Bylund** will lead a workshop to explore this topic on Thursday, **April 19, 7:30–9:00 p.m.** This workshop will cover readiness factors, how to evaluate your child's strengths and weaknesses and a discussion of how to assess the appropriateness of the kindergarten curriculum for your child's needs. Please register in advance.

Workshop registration information

Advance registration is required for all these workshops. 685-1409. Limited child care is available as a service to families with no other alternatives. The fee for child care is $5 and you must **pay in advance** to secure a child care reservation; scholarships are available. **Please be on time to the workshops;** latecomers make things difficult for everyone.

2

Another document gets the round treatment. Note the page heading, initial capital and accent type. The very wide column of the original has been divided into three to loosen the look, and the gray boxes (angular) are eliminated. Square *ballot boxes* have been replaced with circles; note the dotted dividing line.

BANANAS' PUBLICATION LIST

BANANAS is a free child care resource, referral and support service for parents and child care providers in northern Alameda County. In addition to our telephone and in-person services, the staff at BANANAS enjoys providing information, ideas and suggestions through a variety of publications. Please use this form to order those Handouts which appeal to you.

FREE HANDOUTS: All our topics are chosen in response to your requests and concerns. Our Handouts are written in a straightforward, brief style and are designed to be extremely practical and realistic. We try to offer suggestions which may help people decide what is best for their own family or how to approach some particular problem differently. Our current Handouts are listed below by category. Since we began writing Handouts over fifteen years ago, the list has been steadily growing and changing. Free copies are available to anyone living in our service territory of northern Alameda County. Out-of-area residents are asked to contribute 25¢ per Handout to help us cover our costs. Please check the publications you want and send one stamp for every three Handouts you order. Mail to BANANAS, 6501 Telegraph Avenue, Oakland, CA 94609.

Child Care Handouts

Choosing Family Day Care: Questions to ask yourself while you are looking for child care in a family day care setting.

A Closer Look At Family Day Care Homes Licensed For 12: Additional things for parents to consider about providers licensed for 12.

Choosing A Child Care Center: Some considerations when visiting and selecting center-based care.

Choosing Infant/Toddler Child Care: Child care information especially for the parents of little ones.

Choosing Schoolage Child Care: A look at options [suggestions for latchkey kids.]

[...] For A Child With Special [...parents searching for care.]

[...]hild Care?: An overview of [...] co-ops and shared babysit[...]

[...]neral Information on Child [...]erican child care scene for [...]an or Vietnamese families.

[...]: How to avoid complaints [...] ones you can't.

[...]nd New Beginnings: Pre[...]ing child care situations.

Child Care Issues For Expectant & New Parents: The things new parents need and want to know.

Where And How To Look For A Babysitter To Work In Your Own Home: Pointers for using a caregiver in your home.

Employing Limited English Speaking Caregivers: Ideas to help parents hire and retain caregivers.

Sample Agreement For Parents and Babysitters: Writing an agreement to protect everyone. *(Available in English or Spanish)*

Financial Facts About Babysitters Who Work in Your Home: The nitty-gritty of parental reporting responsibilities brought to you by your friendly state and federal governments.

Guide For Babysitters: How to be a good (great!) babysitter written for teenagers and other beginners.

Employer-Supported Child Care: A general discussion for employers and employees.

Especially For Child Care Providers

How To Get Licensed To Do Family Day Care: Questions and answers on the family day care licensing process. Updated as necessary. *(Available in English, Spanish, Chinese, or Vietnamese)*

Provider-Parent Contract: A discussion of the contents, purposes and requirements of contracts.

[...]ANAS, Inc. • 6501 Telegraph Avenue • Oakland, CA • (415) 658-1409 •

BEFORE

Bananas' Publication List

BANANAS is a free child care resource, referral and support service for parents and child care providers in northern Alameda County. In addition to our telephone and in-person services, the staff at BANANAS enjoys providing information, ideas and suggestions through a variety of publications. Please use this form to order those handouts which appeal to you.

Free handouts All our topics are chosen in response to your requests and concerns. Our handouts are written in a straightforward, brief style and are designed to be extremely practical and realistic. We try to offer suggestions which may help people decide what is best for their own family or how to approach some particular problem differently. Our current handouts are listed below by category. Since we began writing hand- outs over fifteen years ago, the list has been steadily growing and changing. Free copies are available to anyone living in our service territory of northern Alameda County. Out-of-area residents are asked to contribute 25¢ per handout to help us cover our costs. Please check the publications you want and send *one stamp for every three handouts* you order. Mail to: BANANAS, 6501 Telegraph Ave., Oakland, CA 94609.

Child Care Handouts

○ **Choosing Family Day Care** Questions to ask yourself while you are looking for child care in a family day care setting.

○ **A Closer Look At Family Day Care Homes Licensed For 12** Things for parents to consider about providers licensed for 12

○ **Choosing A Child Care Center** Some considerations when visiting and selecting center-based care.

○ **Choosing Infant/Toddler Child Care** Child care information especially for the parents of little ones.

○ **Choosing Schoolage Child Care** A look at options for schoolage care and suggestions for latchkey kids.

○ **Choosing Child Care For A Child With Special Needs** Assistance for parents searching for care.

○ **What Is Alternative Child Care?** An overview of playgroups, exchanges, co-ops and shared babysitting arrangements.

○ **Child Care Options: General Information On Child Care Services** The American child care scene for Spanish, Chinese, Laotian or Vietnamese families.

○ **Child Care Complaints** How to avoid complaints and what to do about the ones you can't.

○ **Changes, Changes, And New Beginnings** Preparing children for changing child care situations

○ **Child Care Issues For Expectant & New Parents** The things new parents need and want to know

○ **Where And How To Look For A Babysitter To Work In Your Own Home** Pointers for using a caregiver in your home

○ **Employing Limited English Speaking Caregivers** Ideas to help parents hire and retain caregivers

○ **Sample Agreement For Parents And Babysitters** Writing an agreement to protect everyone. (Available in English or Spanish)

○ **Financial Facts About Babysitters Who Work In Your Home** The nitty-gritty of parental reporting responsibilities brought to you by your friendly state and federal governments.

○ **Guide For Babysitting** How to be a good (great!) babysitter written for teenagers and other beginners.

Especially For Child Care Providers

○ **How To Get Licensed To Do Family Day Care** Questions & answers on the family day care licensing process. Updated as necessary. (In English, Spanish, Chinese, or Vietnamese)

○ **Provider-Parent Contract** A discussion of the contents, purposes and requirements of contracts.

AFTER

Any page looks cleaner when its type is aligned horizontally. The process is sometimes referred to as *aligning to a grid*, the grid being the leading, or line spacing, value.

The leading of the *Bananas* text is 12 point, or 1 pica. But the headlines—and this isn't unusual—are set on 18-point leading. Because of this, a one-line heading will throw the text that follows off the grid by 6 points. To compensate, adjust the Space after measurement by 6 points. A two-line heading (36 points total leading) puts the text that follows back on the grid.

A two-line heading maintains alignment
Because two lines of 18-point type maintain text alignment, (18 + 18 = 36), no compensation is needed. Add 1 pica Space after to the heading to give breathing room to the line that follows.

A one-line heading goofs it up
With 1 pica of Space after, 12 + 18 + 12 = 42, the type that follows a one-line heading is 6 points off the grid.

Adjust the Space after
Select the heading and change Space after to 0p6.
Although the text is aligned across the page, there are now only 6 points between heading and text, a visible discrepancy. The only solution requires more fiddling: Enter 0p9 Space after for the heading, then select one of the empty lines immediately above it and reduce its leading by 3 points. It's still different from the others, but now no one will notice. You'll speed up subsequent entries a lot by make a special *Style* for each variation.

○ **Child Care Issues For Expectant & New Parents**
The things new parents need and want to know

○ **Where And How To Look For A Babysitter To Work In Your Own Home**
Pointers for using a caregiver in your home

Especially For Child Care Providers

○ **How To Get Licensed To Do Family Day Care**
Questions & answers on the family day care licensing process. Updated as necessary. (In English, Spanish, Chinese, or Vietnamese)

For Care Providers

○ **Provider-Parent Contract**
A discussion of the contents, purposes and requirements of contracts.

For Care Providers

○ **Provider-Parent Contract**
A discussion of the contents, purposes and requirements of contracts.

Smoothing out text wraps

Sure, you can wrap almost anything. But try to show restraint.

Text wraps can be nice to look at, but annoying to read, especially if the wrap is on the left of an object. And, unfortunately, although your layout or word processing program may be happy to wrap type around almost anything, it isn't always handled in the most elegant fashion.

The ability to specify text wraps at all is a relatively new privilege: Before computers, wraps were so expensive to calculate and typeset they were rarely used, and when they were used, they were limited to simple, rectangular shapes. Today, any of us can wrap the most elaborate shapes easily, but more often than not, a simple rectangle is still best.

Around small objects, a left-hand wrap should be rectangular so the beginnings of the lines remain even. Make a circular object slightly larger in the space than you would with a rectangle (as shown here).

If your column is ragged and the object you're wrapping is on the right, set the left standoff closer than normal so the empty space left by the rag will more closely match the column edge. Adjust the fit by eye to leave an even space all around.

In general, avoid wraps that fit small objects like a body suit. Readers tend to perceive text and graphics not as an integrated whole but as separate pieces—*this* is to be read, *that* is to look at. The tighter you intertwine the two (as illustrated here) the more conscious the reader will become of your effort, an effect you do not want.

The occasion to hug a contour is if your graphic is fairly large and—this is important—it has a smooth edge. It's always best to wrap on the right, the side where lines end. If you wrap on the left, a smooth edge is doubly important. A busy reader is occupied with reading, and a contoured wrap will draw his eye. The more uniform and natural you can keep its appearance, the better.

A crisp new design is easy to browse, as well as a point of pride.

How to energize a faceless newsletter

What kind of newsletter, do you suppose, would a group of communications professionals want for itself? Probably one that communicates as well as they do. It would be an attractive newsletter that speaks directly and reflects the style, professionalism and pride they bring to their work.

At the time this newsletter was originally designed, the California community college system included a network of more than 100 taxpayer-supported schools. Its bridge to the public was, and is, maintained by a public relations office on each campus, whose work demands excellent organizational and presentation skills.

The public relations professionals in these offices have their own association, CCPRO, for which a newsletter was created (pictured opposite above). Yet for their own newsletter, the one that keeps their own members up to date, the group has taken a busman's holiday. Gray, faceless and forgettable, *CCPRO News* doesn't speak the language of the professionals it represents. It's disorganized: Vital information is hidden amid fluff.

Like other simple newsletters, this can be organized into two different types of information: editorial and dates. Editorial consists of news and chitchat; dates are for schedules. Visually, each should stand apart from the other. We'll do this with a combination of typestyles, weights, sizes, column widths and tints. The result will be crisp, flexible pages that impart their information quickly and clearly— and one that you'll be happy to leave out on your desk.

ⓒ NEWS

The Newsletter of the Community
College Public Relations Organization

❶

August/September, 1994

▬ PRESIDENT'S CORNER ▬

I hope you were able to take some time this summer to relax and recharge your batteries.

Now that the fall semester is here, we charge forward!

I love the fall season, it's really my favorite time of the year. Everyone comes back to campus invigorated...eager new students are filled with anticipation...the media actually looks to us for a "back to school" story or two...and football (ah, I do love football) is once again America's weekend obsession.

I must admit that I have yet to "come down" from last April's CCPRO conference in Sacramento. It stands as one of the highlights of my 23-year community college marketing/public relations career. Workshop sessions seemed to be right on target, and the networking activities were wonderful.

The workshop that looked at planned (and unplanned) job changes—featuring Stu Van Horn, Henry Kertman, Ann Reed and Mark Wallace—was particularly poignant. The panel's honesty and sincerity was touching. I was particularly moved when members of the audience began to share their employment fears and horror stories with colleagues in the room. It was a powerful moment.

The evaluation forms that you so patiently filled out after each workshop session have proven to be extremely helpful. We've tallied each and every one of them (more than 700), and they've provided CCPRO's board with lots of important data as we begin laying plans for the 1995 conference. Literally dozens [of topics were suggested, and] were su[...]

many of them into our conference schedule.

By the way, if you'd like to receive a summary of findings from the conference evaluations, feel free to give me a buzz (714-432-5725) and I'll be happy to drop one in the mail.

Remember...the 1995 CCPRO conference is set for April 28-30 at the Wyndham Garden Hotel in Costa Mesa. The CCPRO board held its annual summer meeting there in June, and the board members were very impressed with the facility.

The Wyndham is located just five minutes from Orange County's John Wayne Airport. It's directly across the street from South Coast Plaza—one of the nation's leading shopping malls—and is steps away from the Orange County Performing Arts Center and nationally renowned South Coast Repertory Theatre.

We'll have the hotel to ourselves. It's an intimate facility (200 rooms)—highly favored by groups that appear at the Performing Arts Center—with wonderful amenities. It has a workout room, pool and spa, excellent dining facilities, and superb conference accommodations. Most of the hotel's rooms overlook a lovely wooded area with a lake. Enough for the commercial!

I'd like to close this tome with a comment written by one of our newest colleagues on a Sacramento evaluation form. I think it captures the essence of our organization:

"I simply want to thank CCPRO for inviting me to participate in this year's

position have been harrowing. I've been involved in many professional organizations, and I've *never* met such a warm and supportive group of people. Bless you all!"

Mega-dittos from this corner. You are, indeed, an amazing group of people!

Have a great 1994-95 academic year!
Jim Carnett

SAVE THESE DATES

WHAT: *1995 CCPRO CONFERENCE* **❸**
WHEN: April 28-30, 1995
WHERE: Wyndham Garden Hotel, 3350 Avenue of the Arts, Costa Mesa, California

DRIVE IN WORKSHOPS
WHAT: Accountability and Customer Service - Are We Doing Our Best?
WHERE: Santa Rosa Junior College, 1501 Mendocino Ave., Santa Rosa, California
WHEN: Friday, October 21, 1994 10:00 a.m. - 2:00 p.m.
COST: $15.00 - includes lunch
CONTACT: Miriam Root, (916) 741-6726

WHAT: Enrollment, Budgets and Advertising
WHERE: Fresno City College, 1101 E. University Ave., Fresno, California Library Conference Room
WHEN: Friday, October 7, 1994 10:00 a.m. - 3:00 p.m.
COST: $15.00 - includes lunch
CONTACT: Kathy Bonilla, (209) 442-4600

❷

The computer did it

The computer is an amazing machine, but it has the design sense of a sandbag. Visually a blank map, the page at left is what happens when you leave every setting on default. Even the name NEWS (**1**)—which has nothing to do with the design—has no identity. It could be the *Green Bay Go-Kart Company* for all we know.

You want columns of text (**2**) to have a smooth, even appearance like a book or magazine, but set *aligned left* without hyphens, you'll get endings like these that are much too ragged. This is aggravated by blank lines between paragraphs, which leaves the text choppy and fitful. A calendar of events (**3**)—the most important information in this newsletter—should stand out for quick identification and easy reading, but here it disappears into the president's letter, its thin dividing lines squeezed between columns as an afterthought. This absence of visual markers is not only unattractive, it leaves the reader to dig hard for information. It's a little like being told to kiss your sister: Without a compelling reason, a page like this will never be read.

PRO!

NEWSLETTER OF THE COMMUNITY COLLEGE PUBLIC RELATIONS ORGANIZATION

AUGUST/SEPTEMBER, 1994

President's Corner
I hope you were able to take some time this summer to relax and recharge your batteries. Now that fall semester is here, we charge forward!

I must admit I have yet to "come down" from last April's CCPRO conference in Sacramento. It stands as one of the highlights of my 23-year community college marketing/public relations career. Workshop sessions seemed to be right on target, and the networking activities were wonderful.

The workshop that looked at planned and unplanned job changes—featuring Stu Van Horn, Henry Kertman, Ann Reed and Mark Wallace—was particularly poignant. The panel's honesty and sincerity were touching. I was moved when members of the audience began to share their employment fears and horror stories with colleagues in the room. It was a powerful moment.

The evaluation forms you so patiently filled out have given us important data for planning the 1995 conference. Dozens of topics were suggested, and we'll be working many of them into our conference schedule. If you'd like to receive a summary of findings from the conference evaluations, feel free to give me a buzz (714-432-5725) and I'll be happy to mail you one.

The 1995 CCPRO conference is set for April 28-30 at the Wyndham Garden Hotel in Costa Mesa. The Wyndham is five minutes from Orange County's John Wayne Airport, directly across from South Coast Plaza, and steps away from the Orange County Performing Arts Center and South Coast Repertory Theatre. It's an intimate facility (200 rooms) with wonderful amenities: workout room, pool and spa, excellent dining and superb conference accommodations. Most of the hotel's rooms overlook a lovely wooded area with a lake.

I'll close with a comment by one of our newest colleagues, written on an evaluation form. I think it captures the essence of our organization:

"I simply want to thank CCPRO for inviting me to participate in this year's conference. You all are very friendly and helpful. My first three months in the PIO position have been harrowing. I've been involved in many professional organizations, and I've *never* met such a warm and supportive group of people. Bless you all!"

Mega-dittos from this corner. You are, indeed, an amazing group of people! Have a great 1994–95 academic year!
—*Jim Carnett*

Dates

CCPRO Conference
April 28-30, 1995
Wyndham Garden Hotel
3350 Avenue of the Arts
Costa Mesa, CA

Drive-In Workshops

Accountability and Customer Service—Are We Doing Our Best?
Friday, Oct. 21, 1994
10 a.m. to 2 p.m.
Santa Rosa Junior College
1501 Mendocino Ave.
Santa Rosa, CA
Cost: $15, includes lunch
Contact: Miriam Root
(916) 741-6726

Enrollments, Budgets and Advertising
Friday, Oct. 7, 1994
10 a.m. to 3 p.m.
Fresno City College
1101 E. University Ave.
Fresno, CA
Library Conference Room
Cost: $15, includes lunch
Contact: Kathy Bonilla
(209) 442-4600

A quick, professional read

Striking in its clarity, this design succeeds because two kinds of information—editorial and dates—work together while staying apart; the narrow gray columns complement and frame the wide text columns, yet contrast sharply. This contrast is key to helping a reader identify information quickly.

Editorial matter is justified in one wide column, which looks smooth and means you have no decisions to make: The second article begins where the first one ends. Bold headings can be browsed in seconds. Tinted columns do not change from issue to issue. Once you've set it up, this newsletter is easier to produce than the original!

Mondrian-style boxes appear translucent but they're not; just snap them atop one another.

1   An exuberant new name

PRO! is one of those unusually strong acronyms that show up fortuitously now and then. It makes for an excellent new name. Along with its typestyle (Charlemagne) and exclamation point, it projects energy, sophistication and simplicity all at once. Its alternating tints work best on very short names. First, set the name and enclose each letter in a box. To avoid a mechanical look, stretch a box into an adjacent space (middle). Now alternate tints of black and three grays—black should always be first—and reverse every other letter.

Longer names work best if the letters remain one color. Three grays are plenty. Rely on your eye to adjust box widths; every typeface is different.

2   Clarify with contrasts

In addition to the tinted columns (**1**), differences in typestyles, weights and sizes further separate one kind of information from another. Calendar headings (**2**) that appear on every page are 12 points, bold, reversed from a black bar. Event headings (**3**) are 9 points, bold; and listings (**4**) are 9 points, light, but are all members of one type family (Franklin), which keeps the look uniform.

Editorial text and heads are set uniformly in 14-pt. leading. For super easy production, set your vertical ruler to 14 points (in *Preferences*), then turn on *Snap to rulers*.

Keys to this design are its narrow, tinted outside columns that carry only calendar information, and its wide inner columns that carry only editorial. This way the reader always knows at a glance what's what. If your newsletter has no calendar, the narrow columns can be used for something else; just make certain, however, that it's an obviously different *kind* of informa- tion or you'll nullify the effect of the visual marker—sort of like leaving your turn signal blinking, then not turning. Tints run top to bottom whether they're full of text or not. Editorial matter simply runs one article after another. Place photos along the gutters; mug shots should all be one size, landscapes another.

Calendar text all starts at the same point and need not fill its columns.

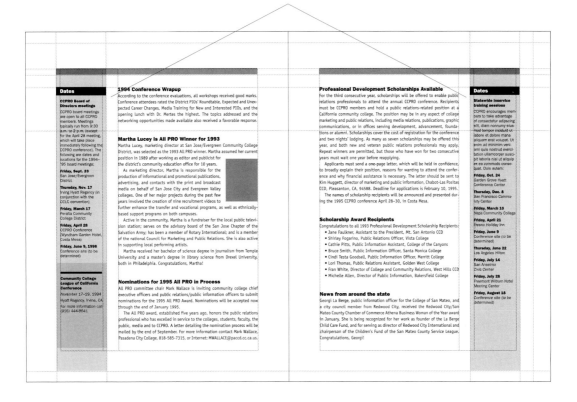

This slick, half-size newsletter can adopt any attitude—from high-tech to antique—and it goes together fast.

A simple, do-anything newsletter

This newsletter solves a common problem: how to organize a page or two of basic information into a tidy package—and quickly. It works well with or without pictures, and with or without a border.

You can experiment freely with variations: The foundation is two columns on half of an 8½ × 11-inch page. These examples are set in just one font—Palatino—but the format will work equally well with about any text typeface you have.

Headline
Always spans two columns. You'll have only one or two of these.

Body copy
Two uncluttered columns. You may add subheads, callouts and initial caps, but they aren't needed in such a small space.

Picture
Comes in two widths: one column and two. If you don't have a picture, don't worry. It will look just fine without.

Border
Optional. Looks just fine without one.

Name
Any fairly short name is suitable.

Caption
After the headline, this is the most important text on the page.

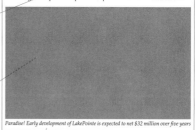

WEEK ENDING AUGUST 19

FORUM

LakePointe Acquisition!

Lorem ipsum dolor sit amet, consec tetuer adipiscing elit, sed diam nonnumy nibh euismod tempor inci dunt ut labore et dolore magna ali quam erat volupat. Ut wisi enim ad minim veniam, quis nostrud exerci tation ullamcorper suscipit laboris nisl ut aliquip ex ea commodo con sequat. Duis autem vel eum irure dolor in hendrerit in vulputate velit esse consequat. Vel illum dolore eu feugiat nul la facilisi at vero eos et accusam et ius to odio dignissim qui blandit prae

sent luptatum zzril delen it aigue duos do lore et molestias exceptur sint occaecat cupiditat nonsimil pro vident tempor sunt in culpa qui officia deserunt mollit anium ib est abor um et dolor fuga. Et harumd dereud facilis est er expedit distinct. Nam liber tempor cum soluta nobis eligend option congue nihil impediet doming id quod maxim placeat facer possim omnis voluptas assumenda est, omnis repellend. Temporibud auteui quinusd et aur office debit aut tum

Paradise! Early development of LakePointe is expected to net $32 million over five years

sectuter adipiscing elit, sed diam nonnumy nibh euismod tempor inci dunt ut labore et dolore magna ali quam erat volutpat. Ut wisi enim ad minim veniam, quis nostrud exerci tation ullamcorper laboris nisl ut aliquip ex ea commodo con sequat. Duis autem vel eum irure dolor in henderit in vulputate esse consequat.

Vel illum dolore eu feugiat nulla facilisi at vero eos et accusam et ius to odio dignissim qui blandit prae sent luptatum zzril delenit aigue duos de lore et molestias excepturi sint occae cat cupiditat non simil pro vident

tempor sunt in culpa qui officia dese runt mollit anium ib est abor um et dolor fuga. Et harumd dereud facilis est er expedit distinct. Nam liber tempor cum soluta nobis eligend op tion congue nihil impediet doming id quod maxim placeat facer omnis voluptas assumenda est, repellend.

Temporibud auteui quinusd et aur office debit aut tum rerum necessit atib saepe eveniet ut er molestia non recusand. Itaque earud rerum hic ten tury sapiente delectus au aut prefer zim endis dolorib asperiore repellat. Hanc ego cum tene senteniam, quid.

adipiscing elit, sed diam nonummy nibh euismod incidunt dolore magna aliquam erat volutpat.

Ut wisi enim ad minim veniam, quis nostrud exerci tation ullamcor per suscipit laboris nisl ut aliquip ex ea commodo consequat. Duis autem vel eum iriure dolor in hendrerit in vulputate velit esse molestie conse quat, vel illum dolore eu feugiat faci lisis at vero eros et accumsan et iusto odio dignissim qui blandit praesent luptatum zzril delenit augue duis do lore te feugait nulla facilisi. Lorem ip sum dolor sit amet, consectetuer Duis

Fuller's Debut Sensational

By Kendra Jones—Lorem ipsum dol or sit amet, consectetuer adipiscing elit, sed diam nonummy nibh euis mod incidunt ut dolore magna ali quam erat volutpat. Ut wisi enim ad minim veniam, quis nostrud exerci tation ullamcorper suscipit laboris nisl ut aliquip ex ea commodo conse quat. Duis autem vel eum iriure dolor in hendrerit in vulputate velit esse molestie consequat, vel illum dolore eu feugiat nulla facilisis at vero eros et accumsan et iusto odio dignissim qui blandit praesent luptatum zzril delenit augue duis dolore te feugait nulla facilisi. Lorem ipsum dolor sit amet, consectetuer adipiscing elit, sed diam nonummy nibh euismod inci dunt ut dolore magna aliquam erat volutpat. Ut wisi enim ad minim veniam, quis nostrud exerci tation ul lamcorper suscipit laboris nisl ut ali quip ex ea commodo consequat.

Duis autem vel eum iriure dolor in hendrerit in vulputate velit esse

molestie consequat, vel illum dolore eu feugiat nulla facilisis at vero eros et accumsan et iusto odio dignissim qui blandit praesent luptatum zzril delenit augue duis dolore te feugait nulla facilisi. Nam liber tempor cum soluta nobis eleifend option congue nihil imperdiet doming id quod mazim placerat facer possim assum. Lorem ipsum dolor sit amet, consec tetuer adipiscing elit, sed diam nonu my nibh euismod incidunt ut do lore magna aliquam erat volutpat. Ut wisi enim ad minim veniam, quis nostrud exerci tation ullamcorper suscipit la boris nisl ut aliquip ex ea commodo consequat. Duis autem vel eum iriure dolor in hendrerit in vulputate velit esse molestie consequat, vel illum do lore eu feugiat nulla facilisis at vero eros et accumsan et iusto odio dignis sim qui blandit praesent luptatum zzril delenit augue duis dolore te feugait nulla facilisi. Lorem ipsum dolor sit amet, consectetuer

autem vel eum iriure dolor in hendre rit in vulputate velit esse consequat, vel illum do lore et nulla facilisi.

Lorem ipsum dolor sit amet, con sectetuer adipiscing elit, sed diam nonummy nibh euismod incidunt ut dolore magna aliquam erat volutpat. Ut wisi enim ad minim veniam, quis nostrud exerci tation ullamcorper suscipit laboris nisl ut aliquip ex ea commodo consequat. Duis autem vel putate velit esse molestie consequat, vel illum dolore eu feugiat nulla facilisis at vero eros et accumsan et iusto odio dignissim qui blandit lup-

Inside Headline
Identical in size and width to the first one.

Byline
The author's name. It can be here or at the end.

The newsletter is laid out sideways on a letter-size sheet, a lively format for any news-letter and ideal for an in-house—or even a personal—newsletter.

Four pages (1 sheet)

| 4 | 1 | | 2 | 3 |

Eight pages (2 sheets)

| 8 | 1 | | 2 | 7 |

| 6 | 3 | | 4 | 5 |

WEEK ENDING AUGUST 19

FORUM

LakePointe Acquisition!

Lorem ipsum dolor sit amet, consec tetuer adipiscing elit, sed diam non-numy nibh euismod tempor inci dunt ut labore et dolore magna ali quam erat volupat. Ut wisi enim ad minim veniam, quis nostrud exerci tation ullamcorper suscipit laboris nisl ut aliquip ex ea commodo con sequat. Duis autem vel eum irure dolor in henderit in vulputate velit esse conse-quat. Vel illum dolore eu feugiat nul la facilisi at vero eos et accusam et ius to odio dignissim qui blandit prae

sent luptatum zzril delen it aigue duos do lore et molestias exceptur sint occaecat cupidat nonsimil pro vident tempor sunt in culpa qui offi-cia deserunt mollit anium ib est abor um et dolor fuga. Et harumd dereud facilis est er expedit distinct. Nam liber tempor cum soluta nobis eligend option congue nihil impediet doming id quod maxim placeat facer possim omnis voluptas assumenda est, omnis repellend. Temporibud auteui quinusd et aur office debit aut tum

Paradise! Early development of LakePointe is expected to net $32 million over five years

Dateline Palatino 10/12 align right

3p0 margin for inside pages. Disregard for this page

Right page setup margin 2p0

Right border margin 1p6

Masthead Palatino 111 pt

15-pt space

6-pt ruled line

Headline snaps at 13p0 or other 1p0 increment

Headline Palatino 30/30 centered

0.25-pt rule at 16p0 or other 1p0 increment

Top of text snaps at 17p0 or other 1p0 increment

Body copy Palatino 10/12 align left

Bottoms of text blocks snap at 30p0 or other 1p0 incre-ment

0p9 gap between text block and photo

0p3 gap between photo and caption

Top of caption snaps at 48p0. Bottom snaps at 49p0

Bottom page setup margin 2p0

Bottom border margin 49p6

Caption Palatino 10/12

- If this is a design that you will reuse—and even if you are not sure that you will use it again—set it up and save it as a template. In this way, you set the groundwork for the design only once. It's ready to be called up at a moment's notice.

- To determine how many words your layout will hold, type copy equal to one inch in depth into your template, using the typeface and size you will use in your design. Count how many words are in a single line. Multiply this count by the number of lines in an inch. Now you know how many words are in an inch of depth. Determine how many inches of depth are open for type in your layout; multiply that quantity by the number of words per inch; and you know how many words will fit into your layout.

- Don't use word spaces or tabs for paragraph indents. Use your program's paragraph indent function instead.

- If you produce your articles in a word processing program, save each as a separate file for ease of insertion and layout later.

4 Setting a name

The newsletter name—or nameplate, banner, or masthead—deserves special attention. And unless your newsletter's name is "Forum," it won't fit in exactly the same space and way as our example.

A name of similar length will fit by adjusting its size a few points. But a longer name must be adjusted more dramatically, perhaps set in lowercase type. A very long name—a whole organization's name, for example—won't fit at all. In this case, consider a shorter name as the main title and set the longer name as a smaller subtitle.

Dateline
WEEK OF AUGUST 19

LakePointe Acquisition!

Lorem ipsum dolor sit amet, consec tetuer adipiscing elit, sed diam nonnumy nibh euismod tempor inci dunt ut labore et dolore magna ali quam

duos do lore et molestias exceptur sint occaecat cupiditat non simil pro vident tempor sunt in culpa qui officia deserunt mollit anium ib est abor

Dateline 115 points

IOWA REALTY COALITION
Crossfire!

LakePointe Acquisition

Lorem ipsum dolor sit amet, consec tetuer adipiscing elit, sed diam nonnumy nibh euismod tempor inci dunt ut labore et dolore magna ali quam

duos do lore et molestias exceptur sint occaecat cupiditat non simil pro vident tempor sunt in culpa qui officia deserunt mollit anium ib est abor

Crossfire! 101 points

Setting an elegant name requires finesse

Setting a beautiful name requires two qualities: patience and a little more patience. It's like painting. All names and letter combinations are unique—they're *artwork*—and can't be just plopped into place. Plan to devote a half hour or more in order to set the name just so. The following sequence illustrates how our example was set.

Typed
Select a typestyle; we chose Palatino. Typed justified at 100 points, it didn't fit. After changing the letter spacing to –10 and the minimum letter spacing to –20…

Adjusted…
we extended the text block window or margin a half-pica in each direction, which permitted the name to fit. Letter spacing was perfect, but the name was smaller than desired.

Resized…
So the name was enlarged in one-point increments until it reached 127 point size. As it grew, letters closed tighter. The result was overdone.

Kerned
The point size was backtracked to 111 points. But now the space between *F* and *O* was too tight, so we added kerning. Kerning was tightened between *OR*, *UM*, and also between *RU*.

And finished…
This produced the final, sleek setting. This extra work is worth the trouble. A newsletter name is highly visible, and fine typesetting sets a quality tone immediately.

**Add a dateline
or company name**
We used 10 point, flush right, all caps type. But experiment with your design: Your dateline may look better elsewhere.

Headlines in this design always span two columns and are one line deep.

Be brief; two dozen characters are about the limit for this space. Our design uses 30-point type on 30 points of leading (30/30). You can adjust interletter and interword spacing to squeeze in an extra letter or two.

Rule a 2-pt line 1 pica below previous story.

Drag text block 1 pica below that.

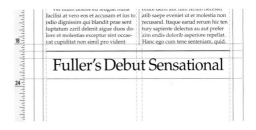

Type headline. Size 30/30, centered. Adjust word and letter spacing if necessary.

Fuller's Debut Sensational

Rule a 0.25 pt. rule 1 pica below bottom of text block. Total depth, rule to rule: 4 picas.

End a story evenly, if possible.

Edit a few words. If *Time* magazine can do it, so can you.

sectetuer adipiscing elit, sed diam nonnumy nibh euismod tempor inci dunt ut labore et dolore magna ali quam erat volupat. Ut wisi enim ad minim veniam, quis nostrud exerci tation ullamcorper laboris nisl ut aliquip ex ea commodo con sequat. Duis autem vel eum irure dolor in henderit in vulputate esse consequat.

Vel illum dolore eu feugiat nulla facilisi at vero eos et accusam et ius to odio dignissim qui blandit prae sent luptatum zzril delenit aigue duos dolore et molestias exceptur sint occaecat cupiditat non simil pro vident

tempor sunt in culpa qui officia deserunt mollit anium ib est abor um et dolor fuga. Et harumd dereud facilis est er expedit distinct. Nam liber tempor cum soluta nobis eligend option congue nihil impediet doming id quod maxim placeat facer omnis voluptas assumenda est, repellend.

Temporibud auteui quinusd et aur office debit aut tum rerum necessit atib saepe eveniet ut er molestia non recusand. Itaque earud rerum hic ten tury sapiente delectus au aut prefer zim endis dolorib asperiore repellat.

Text columns on a page should have the same number of lines. Edit to shorten or lengthen...

sectetuer adipiscing elit, sed diam nonnumy nibh euismod tempor inci dunt ut labore et dolore magna ali quam erat volupat. Ut wisi enim ad minim veniam, quis nostrud exerci tation ullamcorper laboris nisl ut aliquip ex ea commodo con sequat. Duis autem vel eum irure dolor in henderit in vulputate esse consequat.

Vel illum dolore eu feugiat nulla odio dignissim qui blandit prae sent luptatum zzril delenit aigue duos dolore et molestias exceptur sint occaecat cupiditat non simil pro vident

tempor sunt in culpa qui officia deserunt mollit anium ib est abor um et dolor fuga. Et harumd dereud facilis est er expedit distinct. Nam liber tempor cum soluta nobis eligend option congue nihil impediet doming id quod maxim placeat facer omnis voluptas assumenda est, repellend.

Temporibud auteui quinusd et aur office debit aut tum rerum necessit atib saepe eveniet ut er molestia non recusand. Itaque earud rerum hic ten tury sapiente delectus au aut prefer zim endis dolorib asperiore repellat.

...then move next article 1 pica up or down.

Bylines

Add bylines if you wish. A simple byline blends with the text at the beginning or end of a story.

By Kendra Jones—Lorem upsu dolor sit amet, con setetuer adi elit, sed diam nonumy nibh eu tempor inci dunt ut labore et d

i dunt ut labore et dolora quodra xim placeat facir possim omnis nnumy assumenda est, omnis nusd office.   —*By Kendra Jones*

At the beginning of a story, set the byline in bold, followed by an em dash.

At the end of an article, set the byline in italic, preceded by an em dash. Flush right the byline, or if it won't fit, set the byline on the next line down.

Picture captions

A picture should always be scaled and cropped to fill the width of a column; then snap or align to fill the width of a column.

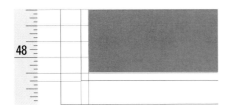

A captionless picture at the bottom of a page should be aligned at 49 picas.

In the cases below, picture placement should be adjusted one-quarter pica.

facilisi at vero eos at a
et ius to odio dignissin
blandit prae sent lupte

The top of a picture beneath text should be snapped to one-quarter pica higher than usual.

Paradise! Early developm

A one-line caption at the bottom of a page should be snapped to 48 picas. The bottom of the picture should be snapped one-quarter pica above it.

President Scott Fuller m

facilisi at vero ios et ac
odio dignissim qui bla

Text beneath a picture caption should be snapped 2 picas below the caption snap.

Picture arrangements

The newsletter does not need a picture to look good—each page is small enough that the text and headlines will look presentable without one. If you only have one picture, place it on the front page unless it belongs to an inside-only article. If you have more than one picture, organize the stories so that only one picture is needed on the front page. More than one might get crowded. Experiment with the following arrangements:

Large pictures should fill their columns fully.

Portrait-shaped pictures should be placed at the top or bottom of a column. Mug shots should normally face into the page.

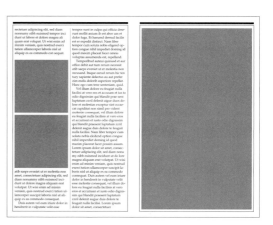

Layouts are almost always more attractive when the pictures are aligned with an edge—top, bottom or side—or grouped, and therefore aligned with each other. The pages of this newsletter are sufficiently small for full-page pictures, too, which can be dramatic. These are often difficult to handle attractively on a full-size sheet.

Book-style layout, legal-size paper

This low-key variation is especially suitable for books, academic papers and other publications intended for a serious audience; that is, an audience that doesn't care for razzle-dazzle. Because its headlines are only one column wide—and it has no ruled borders—it is particularly easy to build; just pour text until a story ends, then start the next one. This example has been set in Garamond 3, a classic font with a literary look.

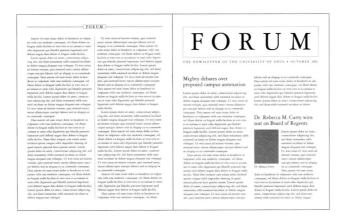

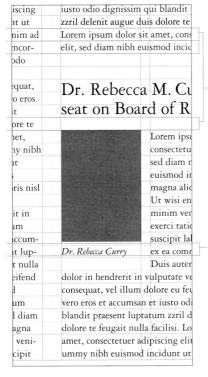

One characteristic of an attractive page is that type aligns across columns, which is achieved here by moving text and objects only in exact 1-pica increments. The two-line headline as shown here should have 1 pica of space after. A one-line headline should have ½ pica of space after to maintain alignment.

Note the quarter-pica adjustment for the picture. The caption must also respect the 1-pica increment convention.

Brochures

How to make a familiar vehicle make a grand entrance anywhere it goes.

Beautiful, square brochure makes a regal impression

Remember the tallest kid in your fourth-grade class? Chances are you do. Why? Because he or she stood out like a lighthouse in a sea of classmates. That's exactly what this brochure does in the mail. Its elegant, square shape folds open to more than 2 feet wide and towers over its smaller companions, causing it to get first

notice—a primary goal in direct-mail marketing. But catching the eye of your audience is not enough. The brochure must be designed to draw the reader in, deliver information with as little fuss as possible, and especially, evoke a response. Here's how to go about it:

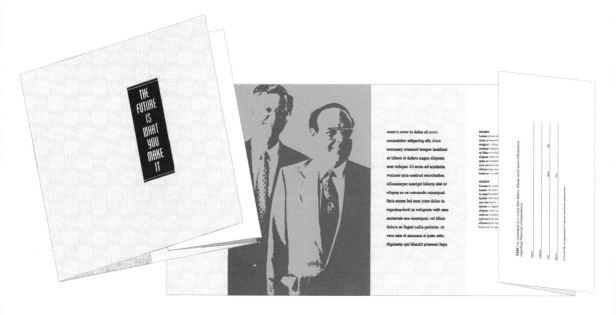

The mechanics

The folds

Handsome, three-panel brochure folds to an 8½-inch square. Far-right panel accordion-folds into the middle and is perforated to make a 4 × 8½-inch reply card. The brochure must be sealed with a sticker to keep it from falling open in the mail.

The paper

Nice, heavy paper will retain the stiff, crisp presence of this brochure's oversize format and make a fine impression on the reader. Ask for an 80-lb. or even 100-lb. *cover*-weight stock. (The folds may need to be scored; your printer will let you know.) If you intend your reply card to be a self-mailer, you'll need at least 80-lb. stock to meet postal service requirements.

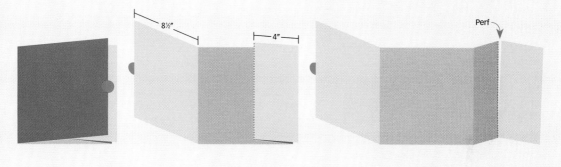

1   Plan your strategy

Our brochure is organized panel by panel in the same sequence as a good sales presentation. It piques the curiosity, introduces the principals, discusses clients' needs, and explains the ways and means by which your company can satisfy those needs. Visually, folds separate the levels.

Page setup

The brochure is composed of three 8½-inch square panels. Total size: 8½ × 25½-inches. For ease of high-resolution output, each panel is treated as one page (dimensions are 51 × 51 picas; double-sided, facing pages; six pages in all; inside and outside margins are 4 picas, top margin is 11p4, and the bottom margin is 5p8; four columns with 3 picas between).

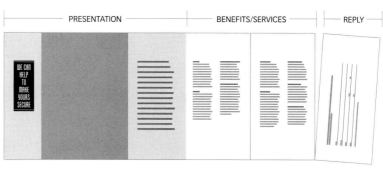

INTRODUCTION   PRESENTATION   BENEFITS/SERVICES   REPLY

What do you say on such a nice cover? A simple, thought-provoking statement is perfect. On a rich stage, the audience will instinctively add value to whatever is said. It's an ideal place for beautiful or unusual typography, too. Note how the box floats serenely in the space. Keep your work simple, though: The format itself carries a lot of the load. If you arouse the reader's curiosity, you've done enough.

A beautiful but light typeface can be made stronger if it appears inside a box.

Just as the typestyle adds personality to your headline, font size and weight set the tone and volume at which it is delivered. Your goal is to match the tone of the type to the content of your message. The four techniques shown here are basic to all typefaces; from large to small, light to bold, note how the volume and tone change.

Add a background image for "texture"

Texture is a printed image—it could be sand or fabric or dry leaves—that almost literally adds a tactile "feel" to your cover. It also transfers its qualities to your message. For example, grainy leather could bring to mind stately offices and ledgers—and the feel, by association, of a successful business. To use texture, look for an image or pattern without a focal point.

While a photograph can make an excellent background texture (center), there are ways to make one yourself. Many programs have excellent custom fills (far left). A logo or a graphic can also be tinted and repeated to create a pattern (right).

Having intrigued the reader on the cover, inside is where you shake hands and walk him or her through your company. And the farther you walk, the more you say. Note the sequence: The leftmost panel makes a verbal introduction (and also establishes *continuity* with the cover statement). The largest panel then introduces the principals visually; the following panel opens your conversation in broad terms, and the small panels fill in the details. Finally, the courtesy reply panel makes a response easy. Each is distinct, yet they blend seamlessly.

A horizontal "hangline" unites the panels

The spare, clean look of the brochure rests on an underlying structure of uniform rows and columns called a *grid*. For this design, the grid is unusually simple: All of the type hangs in columns from a single, horizontal guide. (Note the president's eye level also is at this guide.) Text, set to Align left, flows into vertical columns in the usual way. In the case of the leftmost three panels, the background tints themselves fall on the grid. The text is then narrowed somewhat to fit. Note also that the tints bleed into the gutters. The result gives you a sophisticated-looking set of panel widths that are still governed by the grid.

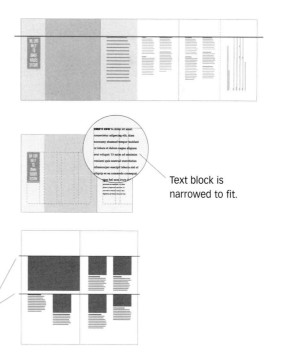

Text block is narrowed to fit.

For a more complex but equally neat layout, just add more hanglines.

This step is magic. Convert a high-res, gray-level scan into one-bit line art, then color it. The result is handsome, inexpensive and very effective artistically. Doubly cool is that by obscuring the detail, the reader sees not good old familiar Joe, as he might appear in a photograph, but the *president*. You've freed Joe's persona from the snapshot.

You'll need photo-retouching software: Some programs' Image control leaves the background opaque so it can't be colored.

Scan your photo at high resolution (400 dpi is enough) at the size you intend to use it.

If you can see a background, mask it and get rid of it. Then convert the photo to a…

…*one-bit* image. Watch the *threshold* setting—it's how you adjust the appearance.

Place the photo onto a flat background (here, 35 percent black) and color it gray (80 percent black).

Monochromatic: Fill the background with a 25 percent tint of the figure color.

High contrast: Fill with solid, opposite primaries: yellow/purple, red/green, blue/orange.

Low contrast: Add 25 percent black to background color and use for figure.

Artistic techniques are easy and colorful

Artwork is the centerpiece of this brochure. What to picture? If your company sells widgets, you can picture widgets. But if your product is intangible, like financial services, you'll have to do something else. Think conceptually, and be creative. You can get the following results with your own camera (35mm or digital is best) in your own office:

PEOPLE

To a reader, people pictures are by far the most compelling. And in a service business, your people really are your product. So put the two together. You can picture key individuals—as you might for a consulting firm—or the whole staff, as you might for a mail-order warehouse. Get everyone together looking groomed, business-like and ready to serve, in normal room light, in front of a plain, light backdrop (about 4 feet in front, to prevent flash shadows). Then shoot from eye level or below. Snap a lot of frames and pay attention to the results; don't hesitate to do it over.

TOOLS OF THE TRADE

This is the "slice of our world" approach. Hunt up objects around the office that represent your business, then compose a still life. Arrange and rearrange freely, but study your progress through the viewfinder. What you want is to establish an *air*, not a literal interpretation. Show a specific or unique piece of equipment only if the viewer will know what it is. Try black-and-white film in normal room light.

NO PHOTO

This is the easiest of all—a flat field of beautiful, bright color can be absolutely stunning. Although the text is only four lines deep, its top and bottom align with the adjacent paragraph (from the hangline). Note, too, that page bars (side and bottom) align with the text.

Typographic detail

To complement your new design, it's crucial that your type observe some professional precepts as well.

Align all text

This design, like most, looks best if the text aligns across all columns—it's a subtle characteristic that separates professional from amateur. The easiest way to ensure alignment is to use one leading measure for small text and subheads (left, 12), and double it for the opening panel (24). At a break, use one full line space. Set vertical ruler to picas, turn on Snap to rulers, and text alignment will be all but automatic.

Type size controls the pace

The design starts with a few words and ends with a lot. Inversely, the type starts big (and spread out) and ends up small (and compact). In this way, the cover and conversational panels appear prominent, and the text-heavy detail panels manageable. Overall effect: an inviting brochure that can be read quickly, with little effort.

Subheads ease reading

Subheads are used to divide big bites into small ones, and to tell readers what they're in for. You can treat a subhead as a mini headline (left), or run it in with text. Either way, set your subheads in a high-contrast typeface (in this case, a bold sans serif). If you don't have one, accentuate the difference by increasing the point size (right).

Fonts used
1. Phenix American, 36/36, all caps, align center.
2. Melior Bold 11/24,with 9-point cap Futura Extra Bold run-in subhead, Align left. 3. Melior 8/12, Align left. Suheads: Futura Extra Bold 8/12, all caps, Align left.
4. Interest line: Melior 10/12, with Futura Extra Bold run-in subhead. Coupon: Melior 7/24.

How to make the most of contrast

Ever wish there were diagnostic tools for design, the same as there are for your car, something you could attach to your design and find out what's wrong? Actually, there are: They're called contrasts.

Contrast is a designer's most powerful communication tool: It can attract the eye, create visual priorities, establish landmarks, control movement, lead, label, emphasize and define. It may be the design secret you have searching for.

Use the following diagnostic tools on your next design. Not every design requires every tool; sometimes one is enough. You'll know which is right for your project.

Value
Contrasts light and dark, negative and positive, solid and tint, colors with black and white.

Quantity
Contrasts many with few, single elements with groupings, often with seldom.

Weight
Contrasts bold with light, mass with line, thick with thin.

Texture
Contrasts tight with loose, airy with dense, smooth with rough, shiny with matte.

Form
Contrasts caps/lowercase, roman/italic, elaborate/simple, square/round.

Scale
Contrasts large with small, tall with short, broad with narrow.

Placement
Contrasts high and low, centered versus left or right, together or apart.

A small but mighty package can be crafted from a standard-size sheet.

Tiny brochure is a great stocking stuffer

This miniature eight-panel brochure is folded down from an 8½ × 14-inch legal-size sheet and printed on just one side. Tuckable into any parcel sent to customers, its "pages" present a short story as they unfold. Its visual simplicity is ideal for a "round" design.

1 Device defines the round space

The problem with *round* is that lines of type aren't round: They're straight. So in small amounts they need some help. The easiest way to help is to center a round device—in this case, the ghost of a putting green vignetted to a soft edge (far right)—upon which type can then be arranged.

In *round*, center is everything. Since round radiates outward evenly in all directions, you must balance your composition across two axes, the vertical *and* the horizontal. To begin, center your device, then compose your headline to fit "roundly" within it (short-long-short).

2 Type alone can define the space

The first inside panel is more complicated. Here, those straight lines of type alone must do the work of creating roundness. Set your type in lowercase (lowercase is much rounder than upper, regardless of typeface and especially in Cheltenham), centered, with tight line leading—lines that are too far apart don't "ball up" properly and look like stripes instead.

Two blocks of copy—a headline and a body of text—together define round. Center your round field and its accompanying "pressure space," then place your (centered) copy in the middle and adjust it outward. Sculpt an edge that's round-*ish*, not razor sharp. To do this, allow a few lines beyond the basic ball (far right).

This format, built entirely from a single, cleverly folded sheet, gives consistency and motion to your message.

Build a brochure with peekaboo panels

This brochure format is like a baby girl—it gets plenty of attention no matter what it's doing—thanks to its eye-catching peekaboo panels. Add the fact that it's easy to set up and inexpensive to print (only one sheet of paper), and you'll find it is well suited for *many* projects.

Begin by choosing between two sheet sizes. The legal size (14 × 8½-inches; folded size 8½ × 3 ⅞-inches) is more convenient; the larger size 14⅓ × 9¼-inches; folded size 9¼ × 4-inches),

in the world of business marketing, is more common. Because of its offset folds, the panel widths vary slightly. Although the amounts will not be noticed by your readers, you will notice them if you attempt to copy, say, a box from one panel to the next—it won't fit exactly!

This is a job for a commercial printer, who should be consulted before you start. Because the folds must be accurate, look for a printer with excellent folding equipment.

Xamplex

Sales and Catalog Services

SALES STAFF WESTERN REGION
HOW TO ORDER

Peekaboo panels...
...make this brochure zesty and set it apart from the crowd. Panel headings lead the reader to the contents inside. Even without the headings, the printed panels are inviting, beckoning the reader to open the brochure. They look very good in shades of gray, too.

You don't need to print the peekaboo panels at all; in that case, use the instructions for Version **B** (see the page specs for each option).

From one sheet with slightly offset folds...   ...fold over...   ...then over again.   Cool.

Page setup (option 1)

14 × 8½-inches (legal-size sheet)

Folded size: 8½ × 3⅞-inches

Handy to lay out and print, this size is well suited to quick, simple projects. Because it leaves empty space inside a No. 10 envelope, it's not quite as impressive to receive *by mail*. Folded *perfectly*, it will fit a No. 9 envelope, a size smaller.

Page specs

Legal size, landscape orientation; 2 pages; Margins: Left, Top, Bottom, 1p6; Right (version A), 3p9 or (version B) 2p9. **Page 1 (Cover side):** guides at 11p3, 11p9, 12p3, 23p6, 32p9, 33p3, 33p9, 43, 52p3, 52p9, 53p3, 62p6 and (version A) 71p7.5, 72p1.5, 72p7.5 or (version B) 72p1.5, 72p7.5, 73p1.5. Four columns, 3p0 gutter. **Page 2 (Back):** vertical guides at 10p3, 10p9, 11p3, 21p6, 30p9, 31p3, 31p9, 41, 50p3, 50p9, 51p3, 60p6 and (version A) 70p7.5, 71p1.5, 71p7.5 or (version B) 71p1.5, 71p7.5, 72p1.5. Four columns, 3p0 gutter between.

FRONT (cover side)

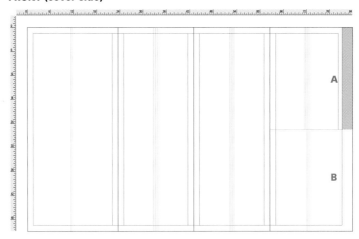

BACK

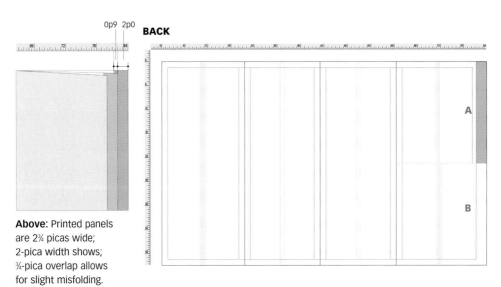

Above: Printed panels are 2¾ picas wide; 2-pica width shows; ¾-pica overlap allows for slight misfolding.

Page setup (option 2)

14⅓ × 9¼-inches

Folded size: 9¼ × 4-inches

This larger size fills a #10 business envelope completely, which contributes to a substantial, business-like impression when received by mail. Printing requires a press that can handle a larger sheet, standard equipment in all but the smallest shops.

Page specs
Page size: 86 × 55p6, landscape orientation; 2 pages. Margins: Left, Top, Bottom, 1p6; Right (version **A**), 3p9 or (version **B**) 2p9. **Page 1 (Cover side):** guides at 11p6, 12, 12p6, 24, 33p6, 34, 34p6, 44, 53p6, 64 and (version **A**) 71p4.5, 71p10.5, 72p4.5 or (version **B**) 71p10.5, 72p4.5, 72p10.5. Four columns, 3p0 gutters. **Page 2 (Back):** Vertical guides at 10p6, 11, 11p6, 22, 31p6, 32, 32p6, 42, 51p6, 52, 52p6, 62 and (version **A**) 72p4.5, 72p10.5, 73p4.5 or (version **B**) 72p10.5, 73p4.5, 73p10.5. Four columns, 3p0 gutters.

FRONT (cover side)

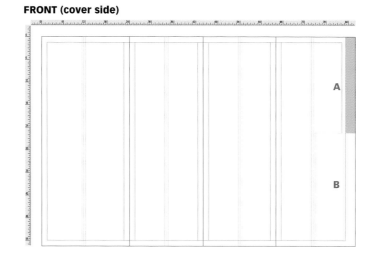

Version A
Use **A** measurements if panels are printed.

BACK

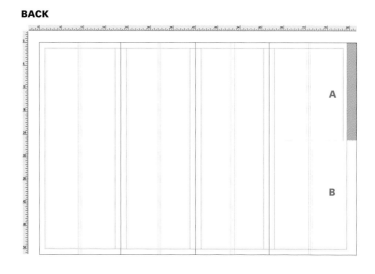

Version B
Use **B** measurements if panels are left blank.

There are umpteen million ways to design a brochure, but it is on a *grid* that good layout begins. A brochure is a virtually blank canvas— no two have ever been alike. The grid will keep you in possession of your sanity by imposing order on your work.

A grid, quite simply, is a set of horizontal and vertical guides, similar to graph paper, upon which text and graphics are placed. On a single brochure, the guides remain in constant position from panel to panel. When designing a *series* of brochures, the guides remain in constant position throughout the series, ensuring a consistent, predictable look.

The vertical guides of a brochure normally correspond to the folding panels. In the following examples, we have also divided each panel in half vertically.

Study the illustrations carefully. We have deliberately laid out diverse and difficult material to convey layout *principles* instead of specific solutions. You will provide those yourself.

A horizontal guide called a *hangline* may be positioned anywhere but typically is one-quarter to one-third of the way down the page. Text and graphics "hang" from a hangline like clothes on a line. A hangline creates an open stage above it and a constant starting point for the material beneath. It is a great organizer.

Horizontal ruler guides may be placed anywhere you wish. These are placed at 1½, 3¼, 12, 13, 18 and 49½ picas. Begin with these, but you must experiment to suit the needs of your project.

The fonts used here are Helvetica Condensed Black and Light oblique.

Horizontal rules are *hanglines*. Text and graphics "hang" from them, like clothes on a line.

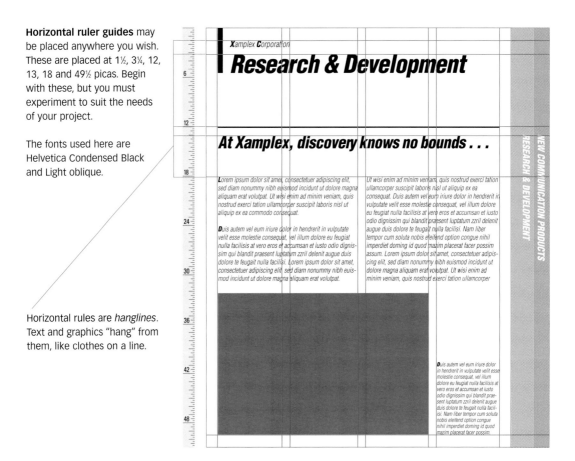

It's simple to create the feeling of family when you keep the same grid and typefaces in place. The iterations are limitless. Inside spreads and back panels are shown on the next page.

FRONT PANEL

FIRST INSIDE PANELS

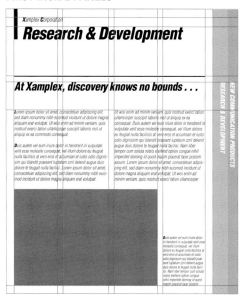

Panel folds are practically invisible and may be ignored. Here, type flows freely across them.

INSIDE PANELS

BACK PANEL

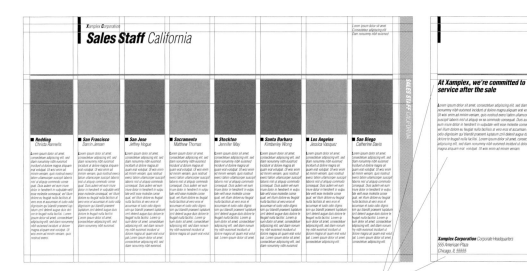

Xamplex Corporation

New Communications Products

No matter what size your company . . . Xamplex has a product that's right!

NEW COMMUNICATION PRODUCTS

Xamplex development ensures your equipment will never be outdated

Xamplex Corporation Corporate Headquarters
555 American Plaza
Chicago, IL 55555

Xamplex Corporation

Sales Staff *California*

SALES STAFF CALIFORNIA

- **Redding**
  Christa Rannells
- **San Francisco**
  Darrin Jensen
- **San Jose**
  Jeffrey Hogue
- **Sacramento**
  Matthew Thomas
- **Stockton**
  Jennifer May
- **Santa Barbara**
  Kimberley Wong
- **Los Angeles**
  Jessica Vasquez
- **San Diego**
  Catherine Davis

At Xamplex, we're committed to service after the sale

Xamplex Corporation Corporate Headquarters
555 American Plaza
Chicago, IL 55555

Back panels are alike—a sign-off head (think of it as an epilogue), closing paragraph and address.

3   Grid intersections are the place to be

Text and graphics are normally placed at grid intersections. If something doesn't fit or look right at one intersection, move it to the next rather than somewhere in between.

Objects are placed at intersections. If an object doesn't look quite right at one, move it to the next.

4   Use empty space as an organizer

The grid can be such a strong governor that *empty space* rather than headlines or font changes can be used to set apart different kinds of information. Once a thought—say, an introduction—is complete, try skipping an entire column before beginning the next.

Empty space creates breaks in the visual flow—there is no need to clutter the page with another head.

Ragged column endings are a useful visual effect; they look sharp yet do not require the same amount of copy for every listing. Be reasonable, however. The layout shown here would be severely compromised if the listing for one salesperson ran into its adjacent column. This is a no-nonsense point: It is nearly impossible to achieve polished visual results if the writing style is undisciplined. It is an area in which desktop publishers have an edge: Often the writer, editor and designer are the same person, so control can be maintained.

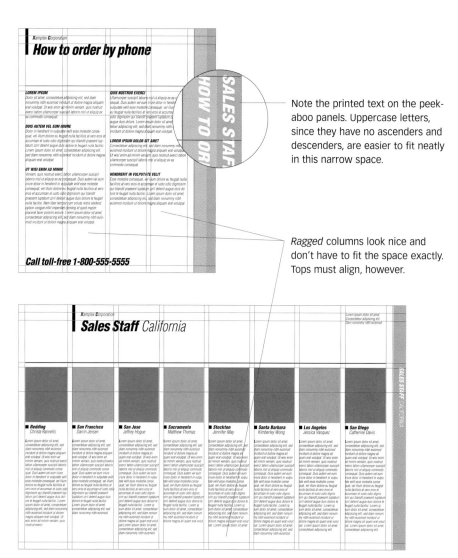

Note the printed text on the peekaboo panels. Uppercase letters, since they have no ascenders and descenders, are easier to fit neatly in this narrow space.

Ragged columns look nice and don't have to fit the space exactly. Tops must align, however.

On the grid: Variations

The grid demands planning and discipline
The empty top-quarter page creates a stage that allows the reader's eye to settle on the heading. This "stage" remains constant throughout the series. Other data begins below the *hangline* at 12 picas.

Three names in eight columns?
Add a graphic, possibly. The California map is an odd shape—as are many graphics—so aligning a black box with the grid and placing the map within it maintain the clean, orderly look of the brochure.

What if you have only five salespeople?
Innovate, but don't leave the grid. Here, an introduction has been written and placed across the two leftmost columns. The larger, bold type, initial *L* and double width notify the reader the information is different.

How about six names and a logo?
The logo was placed into a box, which fills the leftmost column and extends to the edges of the page. The logo aligns with the tops of the pictures. Although the logo is small, the black box and empty column put it on stage.

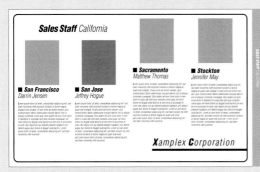

What can happen if you stray
Here, the grid has been abandoned; it has no substance whatsoever. Ironically, the name *Xamplex Corporation* is four times its original size, yet its undisciplined graphic treatment seriously undermines its authority.

An illustrated narrative, a headline, three names...
A second hangline (where the narrative begins) gives the headline breathing room. Double width narrative is distinct from the salespeople's columns. Caption is flush right; empty space above sets it off.

This design is a promotional chameleon, ready to adapt to whatever use you need.

Good-looking pocket brochure works hard, updates easily

If your company or organization has multiple services, a variety of events, or information that changes frequently, this brochure design is perfect. Its heart is a four- or eight-panel folder printed on heavy stock (about business card weight) with a fold-up, triangular pocket. The folder is the static element: Bright and colorful, it conveys your company's image. It's also the only real expense. Into the pocket goes single cards, often just one color, that show services, products, prices, schedules, delivery routes, whatever. The cards can be changed often.

This compact package can be carried in pocket or purse, or mailed inexpensively in a standard No. 10 business envelope. It makes an impression equal to (in many cases, better than) that of more elaborate, full-size brochures at a fraction of the price (a small fraction, too, considering the cost of updates).

Once you've built it and see how utterly convenient it is, you'll wonder how you ever got along without it.

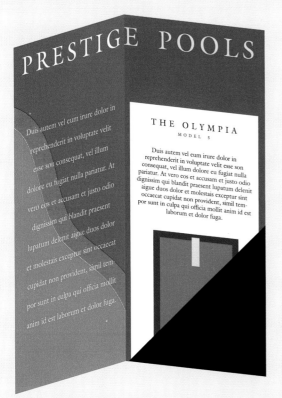

Unbeatable for sales handouts
Full-color inserts are superb for
on-the-spot sales; mix inserts to
match client. It's a handy size, too.
Print inserts at the same time and
on the same paper stock as the
folder for color *and* economy.

Miniature portfolio delights clients
Tiny 8½ × 11's are printed exactly like
normal pages but at 45 percent; high-
resolution film renders even the smallest type crystal clear. For economy, print
minis in one color on an assortment of
uncoated papers. Clients will think they
are adorable.

Four-panel version setup

What follows are three variations of the folder; this four-panel version is the easiest to build and least expensive to print. The inside panels can be left blank, which reduces costs. But you are trying to make a real impression with this design, so you might decide to spend more money on printing the inside and economize somewhere else, such as on your business cards or inserts.

The pocket may be placed on any panel, even on the outside. Refer to the actual size pattern below; once you understand its measurements, you'll find it easy to place the pocket wherever you wish.

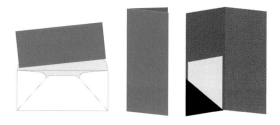

Note corner falls 3 points short of the 24-pica panel width.

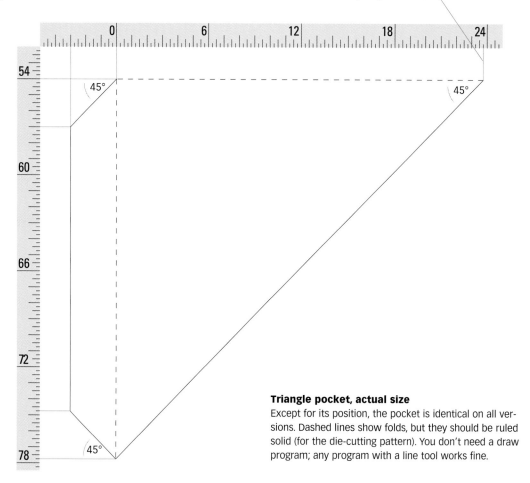

Triangle pocket, actual size
Except for its position, the pocket is identical on all versions. Dashed lines show folds, but they should be ruled solid (for the die-cutting pattern). You don't need a draw program; any program with a line tool works fine.

Set up your document using the page specs given at the right, then follow these steps:

1. Go to the upper-left corner of the master page and zoom to 200 percent. Drag a horizontal ruler guide to 3p0; drag a vertical ruler guide to 6p0, then reposition the zero point to the junction of these guides.

2. Drag vertical ruler guides to –3, 12, 23p9, 24, 24p3, 36, 48, and 51 picas. Drag horizontal ruler guides to 54, 57, 74p9, and 77p9. Rule *corner marks* at the intersections shown. These define the live area and are used by the printer to align the images on the front and back of the sheet (which will be pages 1 and 2 in your document).

3. Turn first to page 3. Create a *die pattern* by ruling 0.25 point lines *exactly* as shown; pay special attention to the pocket detail. Include fold lines. The printer will use this pattern to manufacture a die for stamping.

4. The pattern at right corresponds to the folder's inside panels. Don't forget: For layout, you may find it helpful to copy the pattern to page 1 and rule a mirror image on page 2 (carefully). If you plan to set type on the triangle pocket, it must appear on the *front panel side*, upside down. Once the layout is done, *delete the ruled edges from pages 1 and 2.*

Page specs
Folded size: 4 × 9 inches
Open size: 8 × 9 inches
Printing size (flap flat): 8½ × 12½ inches
Page size: 60 picas × 84 picas, portrait orientation, 3 pages (do not use facing pages).
Margins: Inside, Outside, 7p6; Top: 4p6; Bottom: 28p6. Use 2 columns with 3p0 gutter.

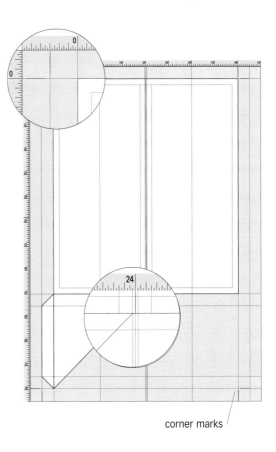

corner marks

Eight-panel version 1 setup

Set up your document using the page specs given on the next page, then follow these steps:

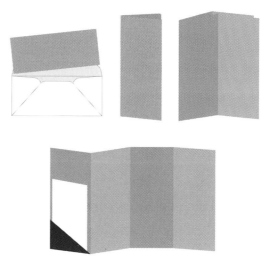

1. Go to the upper-left corner of the master page and zoom to 200 percent. Drag a horizontal ruler guide to 3p0; drag a vertical ruler guide to 6p0, then reposition the zero point to the junction of these guides.

2. Drag vertical ruler guides to –3, 12, 23p9, 24, 36, 48, 60, 72, 72p3, 84, 96, and 99 picas. Drag horizontal ruler guides to 54, 57, 74p9, and 77p9. Rule *corner marks* at the intersections shown. These define the live area and are used by the printer to align the images on the front and back of the sheet (which will be pages 1 and 2 in your document).

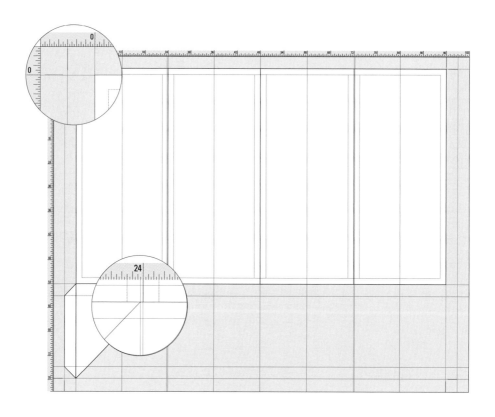

3. Turn first to page 3. Create a *die pattern* by ruling 0.25 point lines *exactly* as shown; pay special attention to the pocket detail. Include fold lines. The printer will use this pattern to manufacture a die for stamping.

4. The pattern opposite corresponds to the folder's inside panels. Don't forget: For layout, you may find it helpful to copy the pattern to page 1 and rule a mirror image on page 2 (carefully). If you plan to set type on the triangle pocket, it must appear on the *front panel side*, upside down. Once the layout is done, *delete the ruled edges from pages 1 and 2.*

Page specs
Folded size: 4 × 9 inches
Open size: 16 × 9 inches
Printing size (flap flat): 12½ × 16½ inches
Page size: 108 picas × 84 picas, landscape orientation, 3 pages (do not use facing pages).
Margins: Inside, Outside, 7p6; Top: 4p6; Bottom: 28p6. Use 4 columns with 3p0 gutter.

Cheery, eight-panel brochure tells a story

This eight-panel configuration is a *storytelling* brochure. Note how each panel reveals the next part of the story. Planned thoughtfully—that is, designed to take advantage of this unique characteristic—it builds anticipation and therefore holds the reader's interest. It can also hold a great deal of information.

If pocket cards are to be printed in color, they look best if they look like the folder, with similar or identical fonts, colors and layouts.

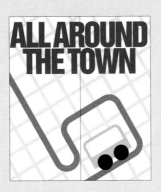

One panel...   **at a time...**   **the story unfolds.**

Eight-panel version 2 setup

Set up your document using the page specs given on the next page, then follow these steps:

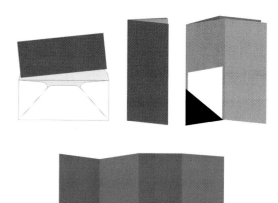

1. Go to the upper-left corner of the master page and zoom to 200 percent. Drag a horizontal ruler guide to 3p0; drag a vertical ruler guide to 3p0, then reposition the zero point to the junction of these guides.

2. Drag vertical ruler guides to 12, 24, 24p3, 36, 45, 48, 51, 60, 71p9, 72, 84, and 96 picas. Drag horizontal ruler guides to 54, 57, 74p9, and 77p9. Rule *corner marks* at the outermost intersections shown. These define the live area and are used by the printer to align the images on the front and back of the sheet.

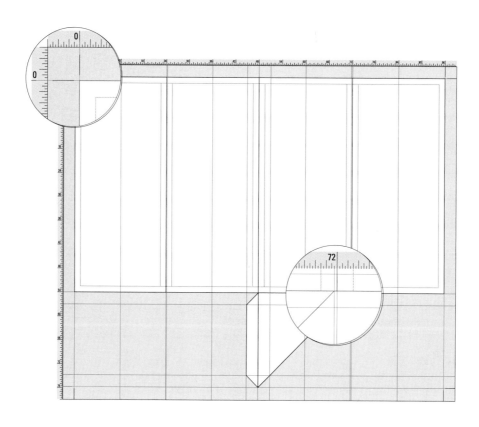

3. Turn first to page 3. Create a *die pattern* by ruling 0.25 point lines *exactly* as shown; pay special attention to the pocket detail. Include fold lines. The printer will use this pattern to manufacture a die for stamping.

4. The pattern opposite corresponds to the folder's inside panels. Don't forget: For layout, you may find it helpful to copy the pattern to page 1 and rule a mirror image on page 2 (carefully). If you plan to set type on the triangle pocket, it must appear on the *front panel side*, upside down. Once the layout is done, *delete the ruled edges from pages 1 and 2.*

Page specs
Folded size: 4 × 9 inches
Open size: 16 × 9 inches
Printing size (flap flat): 12½ × 16 inches
Page size: 102 picas × 84 picas, landscape orientation, 3 pages (do not use facing pages).
Margins: Left, Top, Right: 4p6; Bottom: 28p6. Use 4 columns with 3p0 gutter

How the triangle pocket is made

This brochure is commercially printed, then die-cut (stamped out like a cut cookie) from a single, heavy sheet of paper. Automated equipment then folds the flap and glues the side shut. (Sometimes, people are required for this step.) This process, of course, requires special tools, which will be reflected in the price. Commercial printers have different capabilities; the best price will come from one who has a variety of press sizes and who has done this sort of thing before.

Note that die-cutting leaves extra space on the stamped sheet. You can use this extra space to "piggyback" more printing—for example, you can print business cards or a giveaway bookmark or coupon. You will only pay for the cutting. Your printer can help you plan; you might even consider printing on a larger sheet if the economies are right.

The brochure need not be printed on both sides; it serves well as a blank folder by leaving the inside unprinted. This, too, costs less.

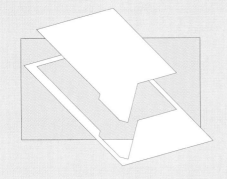

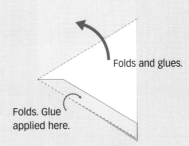

Folds and glues.

Folds. Glue applied here.

Organize and grab your reader's attention at the same time.

An eye-catching zigzag brochure

This handsome brochure will impress your audience and please the budget committee, too. Fancy-looking zigzag tabs are inexpensively made just by folding a diagonally cut sheet. The tabs are highly visible for quick reference and easy reading; print one color on the front, and use another color on the back for the greatest effect. Planned properly, the design fits neatly into a No. 10 business envelope for convenient mailing.

Font specs
Headlines, subheads and initial caps: Lithos Black
Text: Horley Old Style
Coupon: Helvetica Neue Light
Zoo logo: Phosphor

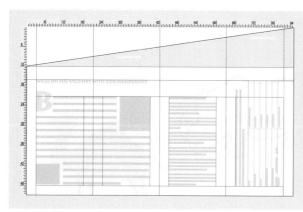

Page setup
Use legal size page (14 × 8½-inch), landscape orientation. Margins: Left and Right: 3p0; Top: 21p0; Bottom: 3p0. Four columns with 6p0 gutter. Set horizontal ruler guides at 12 (to mark angled cut) and 16 picas from top of page. Set vertical ruler guides at 3, 21 (fold), 42 (fold), 63 (fold), and 81 picas.

Those eye-catching zigzags

Note that diagonal tabs are designed separately from the main brochure body. For attractive contrast, reverse the labels (light on dark), then position them to align correctly when folded, with equal space between.

Position labels for correct alignment when folded.

COVER

Reverse labels for contrast.

INSIDE PANELS

1 Animals everywhere

This classy layout makes use of a sophisticated technique: a small color photo and color title (see enlarged cover, previous page) are counter-balanced by oversized but low-contrast clip art. This is opposite the usual arrangement, where expensive color elements get the chief billing.

Color photo and low-contrast clip art balance each other.

Note that elements including tab titles are crisply aligned to an invisible vertical axis.

Background clip art creates a cheerful theme. For best effect, look for imagery that's very simple, then make it very big.

2 Fold like an accordion

An accordion fold is what yields the zigzag tabs and creates this brochure's unusual but very effective two-panels-at-a-time presentation. Fold the sheet in half, then fold each half in half the opposite way.

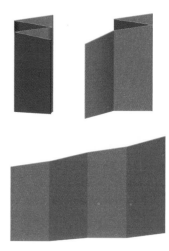

Note how the lion bleeds to the outside edge.

Fliers & Mailers

Follow these steps and improve the vitality of your fliers and mailers.

Preflight checklist for your flier

Is it possible to design a low-budget flier that really sells a product? Yes, if you can keep all eyes on the product.

Imagine walking into a furniture showroom and spotting something you really love. Does your mind immediately turn to thoughts of rentals? What else the company sells? The store's phone number?

Of course not. You want to know more about the prize you just discovered. What is it made of? Will it be practical for me? How can I get it?

That's what your flier must do—show something desirable, tell people why they want it and how they can get it.

The original flier does not do its job well. What's for sale here? A gazebo? Furniture? The item for sale is actually lost in the clutter. The retailer scrupulously avoided hype and carefully provided his store's location, phone number and even a map, but forgot that *the product must come first!*

Let's see how a simple flier can be turned into a powerful sales team member.

AFTER

BEFORE

1 Start by setting the stage

If you think of your sheet of paper as a *theater* stage, you'll be in the right frame of mind. Why? Because a good advertisement is theater: You want to draw all eyes to your product.

Because our product was photographed on a black background, the stage has been darkened to match. This isn't necessary, but it does create a sense of drama, and black is a zero-cost way to get it.

A hairline border frames the stage—think of it as the curtain—and directs the reader's eye inward. Such a border should be subtle; a fat or bright border will draw attention to itself, away from the stage.

2 Place your product front and center

Place your product on a page in the same way that you'd show it off to your friends at a backyard barbeque: Set it smack on the patio where it can be seen and touched.

Picture your product clearly!
To do this properly, you need a photograph. The factory from which your product emerged is often able to furnish a good picture (that's where this one came from). Call or e-mail the company. Failing that, you might hire a photographer who specializes in product photography. This can be an expensive proposition, but remember: If a shopper cannot see your product clearly, *he will not buy it.*

It is tempting to play with a design in an effort to add one's unique signature. Resist! In product advertising, *the product is the show.* Don't tilt the picture or distort it in any way. Don't add ruffles and flourishes. Don't make it tiny, thinking a shopper would prefer to read about it. And don't crop it like an art poster: A shopper will ignore it, or worse, believe you have something to hide.

No!

No!

---

3   Add a headline…

Elucidate! Once your product is on stage, add words to reveal detail and nuance and direct the reader to virtues or uses of the product that are not evident just by looking at it.

Shoppers enjoy seeing and experiencing new products. (We like to be thrilled, basically.) You'll write your best headlines if you think of your readers as eager listeners.

Think: *What is the first thing I would tell my best friends about this product?* Begin with the feature you find most exciting. In this case, it's that although the furniture looks like wicker, it is actually made of durable fiberglass. If your product is more ordinary—a screwdriver, perhaps, or a set of white bath towels—think: *What do I like most about this product? Why would I buy it?* Explain that.

Wicker beautiful.
Fiberglass strong.

Rule of thumb #1:
A short headline is preferable to a long one.
In oral conversation, we yak on and on with 20 words when one or two would do. As listeners, however, we are bored quickly. *Shoppers want to like your product* but they can't tolerate much blather. English is a rich descriptive language; there's usually a perfect word. Finding it will pay off.

Rule of thumb #2:
Avoid catchy slogans.
Why?
1. You won't be able to think one up.
2. If you do, it will be corny.
3. Slogans do not sell products. Would you buy a car because it's a part of "the new generation"? No. You buy a car because it looks good, is well built, is priced right or just plain suits your needs.

As you write your text, bear in mind that a shopper will read it if—but only if—the product and its headline have interested him sufficiently. As you compose it, therefore, *have confidence that this reader is interested.* Keep your eye on the product. Enrich his knowledge. Add detail. Remind him of benefits. Suggest cool uses. Close with a call for action.

Rule of thumb #3:
Be kind.
It is the reader, not you, who is in the driver's seat. No matter how big you are, nothing will happen unless the reader wants it to happen. *Respect that.* A proper advertisement is a dignified product presentation, not a stick-up.

It is an American fantasy to think a shopper can be compelled to buy a product. As shoppers, we actually sell ourselves.

What typestyles?

Always appropriate:
The classics
Understatement—a classic mark of confidence—allows the product to shine. Match headline and text in a font designed for text (the headline should be kerned to tighten it). Some of the best: Times, Century, Garamond, Caslon.

Not so good:
Decoratives
Bauhaus is a heavily styled typeface—part of a class called *decoratives*—whose vigorous presence is a scene-stealer. This diverts the reader from your product. Decoratives are better for posters than product ads.

Cool:
Styles that express their words
Here, beautiful typestyles reflect their words. This technique is best in understatement. It will fail if the connection is obvious (likeliest to occur if the type is bold or very stylized). Remember, the goal is to reinforce the *product.*

TIMES

BAUHAUS HEAVY

SNELL ROUNDHAND, FUTURA HEAVY

Present yourself last—and small. Two reasons: You are the last link in the sale (remember, we shop for products, not stores), and *small* says *confident.*

If you lack a logo, a good alternative is to set your name in a style matching (or similar to) the headline. This low-key treatment makes an implicit connection between the store and *this product*, and is most appropriate for those businesses with narrow product lines: jewelers, florists, specialty boutiques and so forth.

A logo sets a somewhat different tone: It serves as a label and implies that this product is one of a variety carried by the store. Note how the finished flier is divided into four easily digested pieces—headline, photo, text and store name—all of which interact to make a coherent, overall statement.

How to make a text-only logo

In a hurry? Here's a way to make a quick logo:

Gazebos & More!

Typed in Helvetica plain, the name looks... well... plain.

Kern tightly (letters almost touching); remove word spaces alongside the ampersand; reverse type out of a box, and it looks more like an emblem.

Changing the typeface to American Typewriter (note the elaborate ampersand) adds zest—appropriate for a breezy, summer store.

Stacking the type produces a compact look that will fit readily into more layouts. Note that type leading—the space between lines—is extremely tight.

Another option: Take advantage of the computer's ability to generate shades of gray. Type is now bolder; note how the ampersand remains a high-contrast focal point.

Can they find you?

A map is an underused asset. Especially thoughtful of shoppers are maps of labyrinthine parking garages, one-way streets, off-the-beaten-path entryways, things like that. In this case, just finding this small store calls for a sensible map:

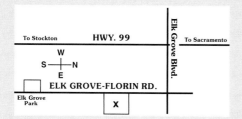

BEFORE: A map made of sticks
This map is the kind one would sketch with a pencil. Its biggest problem? Thin black lines, boxes and large type all look alike and clamor for attention. A reader must spend time just deciphering the symbols! Poor craftsmanship and inconsistent typesetting amplify the noisy instructions. And please, make north up.

AFTER: Gray background, white streets
This way is better—and easier. Rotate north up. Make the background 50 percent gray; set movement corridors in white and buildings in black—this creates high visual contrast between *where you're going* and *how you get there*. Fat streets are the ones you travel on: Typeset names in uppercase (no ascenders or descenders) within them. Streets and their names now function as single units. And delete Elk Grove Park: Except in extreme cases, the only point on a simple map should be the destination.

You can draw all eyes to your product if you properly organize your photos.

Design a product showcase

Photographs are natural storytellers—they are the windows into your company's world. This makes them different from headlines, drawings and other graphic elements that are ordinary and interchangeable. By grouping photos on a page, you can intensify this natural and unique characteristic to great advantage.

Check out the *Before* and *After* versions opposite. On the *After* version, note where your eyes go first. *They go directly to the pictures.*

And what do you read first? *You read the captions.*

The designer is in the driver's seat: The reader is right where we want him.

It is a designer's job not simply to arrange elements aesthetically—as one would arrange flowers—but to *organize information* for the reader. We've done this here by sorting the data into *kinds* and dividing the *After* page into two zones. The light top half carries the story; the dark bottom half presents the products. In this way, we've narrowed the reader's choices, and he is not left to wander about, growing bored.

It is vital, however, to take advantage of the interest we've awakened and speak to the reader *on the spot, in the captions.* How? By turning the captions into complete stories, with heads and even graphics.

New musical realism for the compact disc

The Meridian 208 notches the standard upwards

If ever there were a time to submit yourself to the charms of state-of-the-art componentry, it has to be now. Consider, for example, recent advances in digital technology, which have finally scrubbed away that last stubborn bit of distortion—edginess, audiophiles have called it—from the sound of even top-end CD players. The sensibly-priced, British-made Meridian 208 is our case in point. Actually, it's *two* cases in point—the mechanical (disc transport) and electronic (digital processing) sections occupying their own separate enclosures for superior isolation. The transport glides out to accept your disc, then smoothly stewards it inside, where an air-seal locks out room sounds from disturbing the delicate work of training its precise laser beam on the microscopic code buried just beneath your disc's shiny surface.

Over in the digital processing enclosure, the job of converting digital code into music is entrusted to a new-generation electronic brain called a "bitstream"

Seductive Meridian 208 CD player: At $2,689 save $300.

The Siedle SIC-2000 intercom: A sophisticated bargain at $399.

converter. The sonic improvement afforded by this latest technical feat is absolutely striking on music—orchestral, Broadway, jazz, New Age, soft pop—that relies on nuances to weave its spell. You'll find yourself basking in subtle details that add depth, richness and believability.

The 208 ships with a remote control that is a paragon of clear thinking; how is it that it took all these years for the industry to come up with one so simple and intuitive?

A moment ago we hinted that this is an especially propitious time to consider the upgrade; while (our stocks) offerin(g the Meridian) 208 at ($2,689—a saving of over) $300.

Nakamichi his-and-her clock radio. Alarm clock $199, optional Stereo companion $149.

New musical realism for the compact disc

The Meridian 208 notches the standard upwards

If ever there were a time to submit yourself to the charms of state-of-the-art componentry, it has to be now. Consider, for example, recent advances in digital technology, which have finally scrubbed away that last stubborn bit of distortion—edginess, audiophiles have called it—from the sound of even top-end CD players. The sensibly-priced, British-made Meridian 208 is our case in point. Actually, it's *two* cases in point—the mechanical (disc transport) and electronic (digital processing) sections occupying their own separate enclosures for superior isolation. The transport glides out to accept your disc, then smoothly stewards it inside, where an air-seal locks out room sounds from disturbing the delicate work of training its precise laser beam on the microscopic code buried just beneath your disc's shiny surface.

Over in the digital processing enclosure, the job of converting digital code into music is entrusted to a new-generation electronic brain called a "bitstream" converter. The sonic improvement afforded by this latest technical feat is absolutely striking on music—orchestral, Broadway, jazz, New Age, soft pop—that relies on nuances to weave its spell. You'll find yourself basking in subtle details that add depth, richness and believability.

The 208 ships with a remote control that is a paragon of clear thinking; how is it that it took all these years for the industry to come up with one so simple and intuitive?

A moment ago we hinted that this is an especially propitious time to consider the upgrade; while our stocks hold out, we are offering the Meridian 208 at $2,689—a saving of over $300.

SEDUCTIVE MERIDIAN

Why settle for satisfactory when you can have seduction? The Meridian 208 CD player captures the sonic subtleties that make music magical. The two-box unit comes with a remote control that is intuitive to use—it even rests in the hand nicely.

State of the art intercom

Right: Europeans have always had a more, well, sophisticated idea of how an intercom should work, sound and look. The Siedle SIC 2000 from Germany ($399) is simply the state of the art in all three departments.

Two gentle wakeup calls—one for him, one for her

Below: You can wake up to the tinny blare of a conventional clock radio, or you can have Nakamichi's stereo—his and hers—purr your reveille. Five station presets, bass and treble controls and a true high-fidelity stereo tuner make it a pleasure to face the new day. $199 for the Alarm clock; $149 for the optional Stereo companion.

BEFORE

Don't leave a reader in the dark!

This page doesn't look good—and it doesn't communicate, either. Why? *Because the reader must hunt for a story.* Its earnest but inexperienced designer carefully arranged the page like a dorm room; the sofa in one corner, a chair in the other, coffee table in the middle. He did this because he was thinking *columns* and *borders* and *blocks* when he should have been thinking *story.*

AFTER

Sleek, handsome showcase!

Same pictures, same story, but the photos have been pulled into a showcase, and the results are totally different.

Our *After* illustrates several techniques. Each may be used alone or in combination with others. Some pointers:

Frame your showcase

Here, the gray background is the frame; note it aligns with the text columns above it. A background is usually preferable to a border—it's not as "busy," and it offers more contrast. With no editorial, however, no frame is needed.

Speak on several levels

Different typestyles, sizes, and colors say different things. Such variety is visually engaging and should be used *to presort the information.* To do this, apply styles consistently. For example, captions should all be the same style, color and size (and likewise their headlines), and different from the text.

Think *group*

Cluster your photos in the center of your "showcase" with captions toward the outside— *or* place your photos on the perimeter as shown here, with captions in the middle.

Another headline! This one presorts the captions that follow. The more complete your work, the more successful you'll be.

Longer headlines allow more complete storytelling. Note how the photo breaks the border. It adds action and interest.

Story box mimics page design and typestyles; it's extremely effective at bridging halves of the same page.

Gray background provides a frame.

Photos are clustered on the page for maximum impact.

SEDUCTIVE MERIDIAN

Why settle for satisfactory when you can have seduction? The Meridian 208 CD player captures the sonic subtleties that make music magical. The two-box unit comes with a remote control that is intuitive to use—it even rests in the hand nicely.

The art of the caption

No matter what your subject is, when you group your photos, you create an environment that draws, at least for a moment, a reader's undivided attention. If you consider the antics of advertisers and the fortunes spent (and lost) trying to catch your eye, this achievement is astounding. And it's free.

What next?

You must sell the reader on the spot. To do this, your caption is the most important text on the page. Let's repeat that: The caption is the most important text on the page. It's *where* the reader is looking, and it's about a product that has *already caught his eye*.

Strike *now*.

Write a complete story. Engage the reader with a headline. Ask questions. Solve problems. Challenge. Seduce. Point out benefits. *Sell*—concisely, vividly, with flair. If you are not a writer, hire one.

Headlines on captions provide something to read *immediately*. The simple arrangement shown here is perfectly acceptable.

A 40 percent gray background permits superbold caption headlines to be reversed for eye-catching depth.

Equilibrium affects visual judgment

Our need for balance influences everything we create. Consciously or not, our sense of balance profoundly influences our visual judgments.

The Gestalt principle of equilibrium addresses the stability we seek in everything we see.

In nature, a object tends toward a stable, resting state, as seen in a water droplet. Splashed water beads up—draws inward—and comes to rest in a circle. This is a stable state.

Mimicking nature, we create equilibrium when we draw a plain dot. Like the droplet, a dot is a shape at rest—under no tension. This shape displays equilibrium.

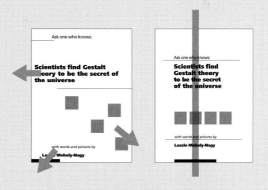

To create equilibrium in a long headline...
Break it into a more contained unit and stabilize it by grouping elements on a common axis.

This fundamental design principle will invigorate your pages.

Make your flier easier to read

A trip to the Renaissance Faire: It's an experience that is rife with flavor and imagination. But it's also an event whose promotion might plunge an unimaginative designer into the land of trite. So it's important to consider your design carefully.

Imagine that for the flier design, you have the fair's logo and a folder full of engravings. With art this cool, you know that your flier will be spectacular.

At least that's what you think. You try one layout idea, then another. You try again. It seems that no matter what you do, the results are basically the same: boring. Even though you're using beautiful art, your layout has no movement. It's static. What's the problem?

Chances are you're not using the design tools of *scale* and *weight* to your advantage. With these powerful devices, you can lead the reader from one element to the next and the next in the sequence you want. Proper use of scale and weight will not only improve your design; it will make your flier easier to read. Let's see how that works.

BEFORE

This layout is orderly but static. The problem: no contrast of scale and weight. Although the pictures and logo are good ones, they are all basically the same size; that is, the same *scale*. In being the same, there is no focal point. This leaves the reader with no visual direction.

The layout could also be improved by greater contrasts of *weight*. Every design element has weight: The darker or bolder a graphic, the "heavier" it is. Squint your eyes at the layout at the right and note the weight of its various parts. With the exception of the text, all the elements have the same weight, which makes for a *blah*, ineffective page.

Experience the Renaissance

Spend this Sunday, November 7, in the 15th century. Consectetuer adipiscing elit, sed diam nonummy nibh euismod tincidunt ut laoreet dolore magna aliquam erat volutpat. Ut wisi enim ad minim veniam, quis nostrud exerci tation ullamcorper suscipit lobortis nisl ut aliquip ex ea commodo consequat. Duis autem vel eum iriure dolor in hendrerit in vulputate velites molestie consequat, vel illum dolore eu feugiat nulla facilis is at ve- roeroset acc umsan et ius- to odio dign- issim qui blan dit praesent luptatum zril delenit augue duis dolore te feugait nulla facili. Lorem ipsum dolor sit amet, con- sectetuer ad-

Stroll amongst the minstrels or watch the knights vie for the attention of damsels.

ipiscing elit, sed diam nonummy nibh euismod tincidunt ut laoreet dolore magna aliquam erat volutpat. Ut wisi enim ad minim veniam, quis nostrud exerci tation ullamcorper suscipit lobor-

tis nisl ut aliquip ex ea commodo consequat. Duis autem vel eum iriure dolor in hendrerit in vulputate velit esse molestie consequat, vel illum dolore eu feugiat nulla facilisis at vero eros et accumsan et iusto odio dignissim qui blandit praesent luptatum zzril delenit augue duis do- lore te feugait nulla facilisi. Nam liber tempor cum soluta nobis eleifend option congue nihil imperdiet doming id quod mazim placerat facer possim freassuman. Lorem ipsum dolore ansit amet, etued.

RENAISSANCE
PLEASURE FAIRE

EXPERIENCE THE RENAISSANCE

Spend this Sunday, November 7, in the 15th century. Consectetu- er adipiscing elit, sed diam nonummy nibh euismod tincidunt ut laoreet dolore magna aliquam erat volutpat. Ut wisi enim ad minim veniam, quis nostrud exerci tation ullamcorper suscipit lobortis nisl ut aliquip ex ea commodo consequat. Duis autem vel eum iriure dolor in hendrerit in vulputate velit esse molestie consequat, vel illum dolore eu feugiat nulla facilisis at vero eros et accumsan et iusto odio dignissim qui blandit praesent lupta- tum zzril delenit augue duis dolore te feugait nulla facilisi.

Lorem ipsum dolor sit amet, consectetuer adipiscing elit, sed diam nonummy nibh euismod tincidunt ut laoreet dolore magna aliquam erat volut- pat. Ut wisi enim ad minim veniam, quis nostrud exerci tation ullamcor- per suscipit lobortis nisl ut aliquip ex ea commodo consequat. Duis autem vel eum iriure dolor in hendrerit in vulpu- tate velit esse molestie consequat, vel illum dolore eu feugiat nulla facilisis at vero eros et accumsan et iusto odio dignis- sim qui blandit praesent luptatum zzril delenit augue duis dolore te feugait nulla facilisi. Nam liber tempor cum soluta nobis eleifend option congue nihil imper- diet doming id quod mazim placerat facer possim freas- suman. Lorem ipsum dolore an- sit amet, etued.

Stroll amongst the minstrels or while away the day watching the knights vie for the attention of the fairest damsels.

RENAISSANCE
PLEASURE FAIRE

AFTER

Much better! Scale and weight are used to their fullest advantage. The result is a lively, inviting flier.

1   Pick one element to be dominant…

…and make it large and/or heavy. Remember, dominance depends on both scale and weight. Something large can actually recede because it has very little weight.

Why a dominant element?
Varying the size and weight of the graphics is how the designer guides the reader around the layout. When the eye scans the page, it sees the biggest or heaviest item first. It then travels to the next-largest element and continues viewing by scale until it has examined the entire page.

The savvy designer will use this to his advantage; he will manipulate the size of the graphics to steer the reader in the desired direction.

In this example, it was determined that the minstrel engraving would be dominant. Note how the remaining elements are scaled to move the eye around the page.

Minstrel image is dominant; numbers show how the eye moves across the page.

Scale the remaining elements…

…so they appear smaller and/or lighter than the dominant one. In most cases, you'll want to create a descending order of scale—something is large, another is mid-sized, another is small. The reader's eye will generally move from one to the next in the order you scale them.

2   Create type contrasts

Use size, weight, or both to create contrasts among headline, text and caption copy. For the headline, bold Compacta was chosen for its very high contrast with the dainty, serif text (Cochin). Its size was then reduced, however, so it would not dominate—or compete for dominance with—the minstrel graphic. For the same reason, a heavy sans serif was chosen for the caption.

Determine your emphasis

As the designer, you are the one who will judge which element will catch the reader's eye. In some cases, you will attract attention with a graphic, other times with a headline (right) and occasionally (below right) with the text. Just be sure that what you want to emphasize is dominant on the page.

Where the headline was selected to be dominant, a lighter weight typeface was substituted. It is very attractive, but only because the headline is very large. If this headline were as small as our original "after," the typeface would have made it appear weak and recessive.

Engravings: A hot old source for art

Tired of that same old clip-art look when putting together your newsletter? Try using old engravings. These finely detailed, turn-of-the-century illustrations lend an added sense of quality to any project. Best of all, they are very inexpensive.

Many companies sell books, CDs or online engraving art; a quick search on the Internet will reveal many sources.

Those who are more adventurous can start their own archive of engravings by haunting used book and antique stores. The collector should be cautious of copyright infringement, however. As a rule of thumb, do not use any artwork that is less than 75 years old.

Scanning tips

Engravings can be tricky to scan. Because they are composed primarily of very fine lines, they have a tendency to fill in and lose detail. Reproducing the image on a copier prior to scanning seems to help. Set the exposure slightly lighter than normal. This intensifies contrast and gives the appearance of increasing resolution. Clean up any blobs on screen electronically or on paper with good old correction fluid.

The artwork should be scanned at 300 dpi at the size you intend to use it. Scans that have been enlarged after they have been placed in a program tend to break up, and the scanning resolution shows itself in the illustration.

For best results, scan the engraving as line art. Increase the brightness to keep the contrast gained from copying. Save the art as a TIFF.

Words *inform*—while art imparts the *feeling*.

Add real feeling to your flier

How can you design fun and casual fliers without ignoring readability or design guidelines?

One of the best ways is with pictures. To do so, first understand how pictures communicate differently than words. Think of words as *information* and pictures as *feeling*. Your goal is to use pictures not to restate the words but to set a mood; that is, to convey what you want your audience to *feel*.

Pictures and words will combine to "broadcast" on many channels at once. Keep in mind that they always work together; a change in one will affect the other. What's fun is that the interaction can yield fruitful surprises. The following four techniques are basic to all picture-word layouts.

BEFORE
What's the matter here?
It's that too much attention has been given to getting attention. The word *attention* tries but isn't strong enough. Yellow paper helps, but makes the effort much too obvious. Let's work on the message first.

This iteration just *feels* good.
What says "casual" better than hanging around? The art says *relax*; the word "casual" feels *casual*. And white paper works just fine.

FRIDAY IS CASUAL DAY

FRIDAY, AUG. 27 • CASUAL DAY AND RECESS!
Meet outside under the pergola at 2 p.m. for recess. Bring your jump rope, ball or whatever else you want to play with. We will have the drawings for the contests as well. Recess will last for one hour, so there's plenty of time for everyone to come down for a while.

We got an *F* on our report card for appearance this last casual day. Please remember that casual day means *professional* casual clothes. We don't want to post hall monitors near the elevators to make sure you're dressed appropriately. We could lose our casual days, so please save the beachwear for the weekends.

HEADLINE: FASHION COMPRESSED AND MYRIAD TILT; TEXT: GARAMOND LIGHT CONDENSED

1   Same size headline and art

How would you inform a colleague about Casual Day? You'd say, "Friday is Casual Day." That's how to write a headline, and it's a great way to start your design. Then what? Find *one* piece of art to characterize your message. To find this one, we keyed on the word *Casual* and thumbed through art until we found a cheery little opossum, who looked like he was enjoying himself—exactly how Casual Day devotees should feel.

Then what? In this case, the headline was set first, and the opossum was hung nearby. After that, placement of the text seemed obvious. Note the wide leading (14/19) and the immense amount of white space. The result is ideal: The headline says it, but the art lets you feel it.

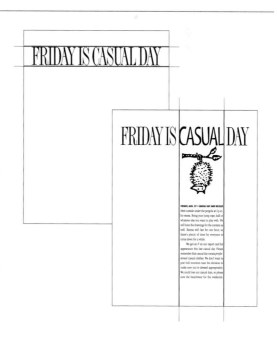

2 Big headline, small art

Here the headline carries the design; the art is now a supporting player. Leading is extremely tight (200/150); an align-left setting has created big gaps into which justified text can be tucked quite neatly. Huge contrasts in type sizes and styles are *sophisticated*. This technique is easy and a lot of fun—and works with many type-faces (below).

(FAR LEFT) HEADLINE: FASHION COMPRESSED; (ABOVE AND LEFT) HEADLINE: FRANKLIN GOTHIC CONDENSED; TEXT: GARAMOND BOOK CONDENSED.

3 Big art, small headline

Art now dominates the design, and the message acquires a hint of wit. Note, far right, that, as with the opossum, the lecturer has no direct connection to Casual Day. Remember, the job of the picture is to create a *feel*. Primitive art requires special typography—balance the ragged style with slick, understated text (right, centered; far right, margin to margin). Note all of the empty space. If you are new to this, try ignoring the column guides and watch instead for lines of sight. If one develops, take advantage of it.

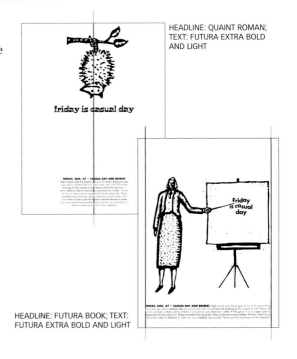

HEADLINE: QUAINT ROMAN; TEXT: FUTURA EXTRA BOLD AND LIGHT

HEADLINE: FUTURA BOOK; TEXT: FUTURA EXTRA BOLD AND LIGHT

What a difference a headline can make. Here a detached pronouncement—RAFFLE TO HELP FLOOD VICTIMS IN THE MID-WEST—has been replaced with WIN A PAIR OF ROCKIES TICKETS!, which shifts the attention from *them* to *me*. We'll get to *them* in a moment; in the meantime, the booming typestyle generates a *feeling* of excitement. We have now gained the reader's ear, into which we can plead our case to great effect. (Note "various baked goods" have also been recast into desirable prizes.) If you have a lot to say, especially if it's central to the message, set your text quite large (here, 20/21)—which makes it easier to read and elevates its value—then sprinkle in clip art as seasoning. In this case, the art's purpose is to provide visual reinforcement. You'll get good results most easily if the clip art is all one style. Note here that the art illustrates the words literally.

Raffle BEFORE

Raffle AFTER

WIN A PAIR OF ROCKIES TICKETS!

Join us in a raffle to help victims of the floods

Victims of the great floods have suffered terrible losses. *Let's do something to help.* A mere $1 contribution can win a pair of Rockies tickets (we have *two* pair to give away!) or some of the most delicious, made-with-loving-care baked goods you've ever tasted. Tickets will go on sale Monday, **July 26.** Drawings will be held Friday, **July 30,** at 2 p.m. under the pergola. Please be generous. *Great West will add a lump-sum donation to what we raise from the raffle.* All money raised will be donated to the Red Cross. • We need ten very special volunteers to provide the baked goods. If you can contribute with your oven instead of your wallet, please call Susan Seibel on 3992.

Buy your tickets from any of the following Catch the Spirit coordinators: Jan O'Malley (4078), Susan Seibel (3992), Sarah Withers (4270), Leslie Layman (3956), Gity Prout (4169), Robin Gugel (4456), Marcel Grenier (3148), Kelly Williams (4113), Marybeth Daubenspeck (5359), Garry Edwards (5057), Juanita Ringor (3215).

HEADLINE: FUTURA EXTRA BOLD CONDENSED; TEXT: ITC CENTURY BOOK CONDENSED

The customer is king with this generous coupon card.

A greeting with a surprise

In a world where service is so often wanting, a gesture like this coupon card is all the more memorable. This version acknowledges a new customer, offers a credit toward the next purchase, and extends a welcome from the company president. You can present it when you first do business with a customer or mail it as a follow-up.

The gray screen (here 10 percent) on the inside panels adds visual contrast between the coupon and the card. The gray horizontal lines represent folds.

To print this in your office (but with no bleed), set it up as a two-page document (6 × 11-inches) and manually feed your laser printer, head-first on one side, tail-first on the back side. For heavier stock (65-lb. is ideal) or large quantities, take the job to a commercial printer to have it mass produced, perforated and machine-folded.

This triple-panel production pops the payoff to your headline.

A magic message

Magicians call it misdirection. You're confident you know exactly what you're looking at and then suddenly, a rabbit pops out of a hat. The same is true with this triple-panel pop-up. A provocative headline draws your reader in and *presto!*—up pops your company name, your phone number or your call to action.

The layout fits within a standard 8½ × 14-inch legal sheet. If you need more than a few copies, your local commercial printer can print, score, and die-cut the mailer. Be sure to specify, at minimum, an 80-lb. cover stock. If you need only a few copies and your laser printer can

handle heavy stock, you can cut the slots and score it yourself. Try using a straightedge and a dinner knife or letter opener to score the folds.

The finished pieces is sized to fit an A2 or 4⅜ × 5¾-inch envelope.

Triple panel pop-up layout
1 Headline: Franklin Gothic Heavy, 42/36-pt., align center; **2 Pop-up headline:** Franklin Gothic Heavy, 65-pt., align center; **Pop-up subhead:** Century Expanded, 17-pt., align center; **3 Text:** Century Expanded, 17/20-pt., align center

If you're making five figures ❶

and you've set your sights on six figures

you need these seven figures

654-3210 ❷

area code 987

Sampler Professional Search ❸

We recruit and place professionals in banking, healthcare and high technology. If you're interested in reviewing our current portfolio of opportunities or you would like to learn more about our career counseling services, please call at your earliest convenience.

A table tent takes a 2-D message into the 3-D world.

A flier that stands on its own

Ever sit in a restaurant reading the signs on the table? With little else to focus on, many clients and customers bide their time by reading. What an opportunity! Big advertisers pay millions for such an attentive audience. Play your cards right, and you can have it for pennies.

The example shown here is an plea seeking county fair exhibitors. It might be displayed in a restaurant, at a 4-H meeting, or in a crafts class. Or you might fold it into a business envelope and send it to a list of last year's exhibitors.

Prescored table tent sheets are available from office supply stores, but this design can accomplish the same effect for next to nothing. Print your 3-D flier on 80-lb. cover stock, and score it with a metal ruler or butter knife. A commercial printer should be contacted for longer print runs; the printer can also attach a strip of double-sided tape to the tab on the right. When you are ready to assemble the finished piece, simply expose the tape and connect the sides.

Places to put your table tents: cafeterias, check-out counters, hotel rooms, laundries, libraries, restaurants and bars, waiting rooms.

Table tent layout
1 Subhead: Times New Roman italic, 16-pt., align center; **2 Headline:** Racer, 175-pt., align center; **3 Text:** Times New Roman, 16/18-pt., aligned left (text below, align center); **4 Art:** dingbat font, 180-pt., align center

Sampler County Fair

NOW

Now is the time to prepare your entries for the Sampler County Fair, to be held between September 22 and October 2 of 1998. Exhibit categories include:

Agricultural Crops
Flowers
Home Arts
Horses
Livestock
Youth Arts & Crafts

Sampler County Fair

HOW

How do you get involved? Call or write for a complete Fair Exhibitor's Package including the programs, itinerary, premium listing, general rules, entry forms and ticket information:

987-654-3210

Sampler County Fair
P.O. Box 12345
Your City, ST 12345-6789

Sampler County Fair

WOW

The seventy-second annual Sampler County Fair is sure to be the best yet. You'll see the finest our county has to offer and experience some good family fun. Your $10 admission ticket includes:

Fair Exhibits
Sampler Heritage Village
Nightly Fireworks
Rides
Nightly Rodeo

Create an unforgettable mailer, one that sails into readers' hearts.

A flying flier

Whoever receives this "flying flier" will be able to fold it into a great-looking airplane and be delighted in about a minute. What makes it so easy is a series of strategically placed numbers; the recipient folds the numbers face to face, and it's ready for take-off. The obvious benefit to you is that this irresistible puzzle gets your prospect totally involved with your message.

You begin by re-creating the pages shown here as accurately as possible on a standard 8½ × 11-inch sheet—fold lines, numbers, and instructions—everything but your marketing message and the blue grid lines (the half-inch grid shows you exactly where to position the numbers).

Once you have all of the numbers and lines in place, you can place your message as shown or study where each part of the page ends up on the folded plane and design your own—the sky's the limit.

The marketing challenge is to link your message to the airplane metaphor (such as "plane and simple") using the basics of any successful direct-mail piece—informative text, an attractive offer, and an obvious, easy way to respond. Print the final version on high-quality, letter-weight stock and hand it out, mail it flat, or fold it like a letter and deliver it in a standard No. 10 business envelope.

A truly great plane is beautifully simple. ❶

With expert help, problems have a way of turning into solutions. Sampler Water Works has been designing and installing water treatment systems since 1984. ❷ Call us at 987-654-3210 and we'll show you the difference between a plan that flies and one that doesn't.

Folding instructions:
Place on a flat surface with this text facing you. Now simply fold the sheet so that like numbers connect face to face. For example, when you connect the number ① on the right with the number ① on the left, you automatically create a fold from top to bottom. Connect all the numbers, front and back.

Staple here when finished

❸

Folding instructions:
Place on a flat surface with this text facing you. Now simply fold the sheet so that like numbers connect face to face. For example, when you connect the number ① on the right with the number ① on the left, you automatically create a fold from top to bottom. Connect all the numbers, front and back.

❹

❺

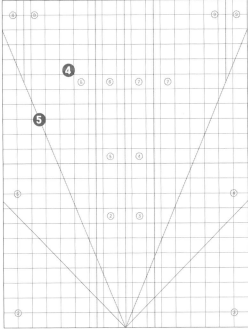

Paper airplane
1 Headline: Garamond Light Condensed, 45/39-pt., align right; Letter "e": 40 percent tint of black;
2 Text: Garamond Light Condensed, 17/16.5-pt., align left; Bold text: Franklin Gothic Book Condensed, 15/16.5-pt., align left; **3 Instructions headline:** Franklin Gothic Book Condensed, 8/9-pt., align center; Instruction text: Franklin Gothic, 8/9-pt., align center; **4 Numbers:** Franklin Gothic Condensed, 12-pt., align center; Circle line: .5-pt., 40 percent tint of black; **5 Lines:** .5-pt, 40 percent tint of black

Want to wish customers your best? Send them a card.

A miniature postcard

Does your business involve tourists or visitors?
Why not send them on their way with this efficient business card postcard? A full-color photo
on one side is a beautiful reminder of a pleasant stay. On the other are your name, address,
phone and fax—all the business card standards
for easy planning of a return trip or repeat stay.
A tiny 9 × 12-inch press sheet can hold a dozen
different images for inexpensive, season-to-
season variety.

Specs
Card 1, Palatino. **Card 2**, Vendrome (for SunTours)
and Copperplate Condensed (address).

Advertising

Getting the balance just right is easier than you might think.

How to lay out a good advertisement

A foundation of page space roughly divided into three-fourths picture, one-fourth other material—mostly text—is the most successful format in advertising. Check out any publication that carries advertising, and you'll quickly see that this is true. Among its strengths, it encourages the designer to build a story by arranging elements in a linear sequence—picture, then headline, then text, then logo.

In the airy world of artistic expression—that savannah of beautiful trademarks, elegant brochures and soaring ideals—commercial advertising swings a brick bat. Here is the big league. Hardball. The maker and mover of financial titans.

How is it different? It is that to *sell*, a designer must *communicate*, not merely beautify. On a tiny stage without motion or sound, it is your job to craft a visual message that will arrest a total stranger and enchant him so completely that he will empty his wallet into your client's hands.

There are ways to do this.

First lesson: There exists one format more universally suited to the task than any other. Big or small, tall or wide, in a newspaper or the phone book, this layout will cut the clutter, take center stage, tell your story and deliver a response. Let's have a look.

Divide the space, then build your ad one element at a time

This format helps you organize your ideas and state them plainly. It does this by reducing an ad to four basic and *clearly delineated parts:*

1. Picture
2. Headline
3. Text
4. Logo

Assemble it step by step and don't let its simplicity fool you: This format is a powerhouse.

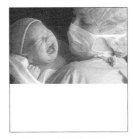

1. Place the picture...
Put it at the top. Touch the edges.

2. then the headline...
Use pure, clear type. Don't decorate.

3. then the text...
Serif type, always. It's what we read best.

4. then the logo.
The punctuation mark. A full stop.

Any shape will do
Thirds and quarters are best, but don't lose sleep over exact divisions.

Vertical format is just as useful

Divide the space vertically instead—the principles are the same. How to decide? The shape of your picture and the length of your headline will dictate.

It's surprisingly easy: Just show us the stuff!

How to design a powerful product ad

We shoppers love to see new stuff! If you have a product to sell, there is no hook more alluring than to simply show it off naturally so that it looks like it does in the store.

To do this best, you need color, whether it is inkjet-, laser- or offset-printed. Any piece printed in color garners more attention.

Being able to print color in the office is good news. It means we can bring the clout of professional design to everything we sell. The display techniques that work for Madison Avenue will work for us, too.

To see how, follow the design of a thoroughly modern flier to sell a good, secondhand bike.

1   Wheel it in

In real life, how would you show off your bike to a friend? It's easy—you'd wheel it right in and point out the cool parts. That's exactly what you'll do here. First scale your photo up, up, up, large enough to see life-size. Only have a skinny space available? Then crop, rather than shrink, your shot.

2   State your business

Write a headline that states your business, and set it simply. Note how natural the presentation appears? Visualize yourself as the shopper. Ask, *what would I want to know?*

For Sale: Paramount/Dura-Ace

1988 62cm handbuilt Paramount. $1099

TYPEFACES: FRANKLIN GOTHIC CONDENSED, CENTURY OLD STYLE

Lead the shopper around your product and tell him what he's looking at. Callouts do a great job of holding attention—you read, then look; read, then look. In this case, we label but don't elaborate; the shopper will already be familiar with the significance of the bike's parts. In another case we would: With the photo holding the viewer's attention, a sentence or two near each part could be quite engaging. Your decision will depend partly on how well your product is known.

The short narrative provides an important human touch. It's where we talk. Remind the shopper of the bike's value, provide some history, and give him a way to take action. It has another benefit: It keeps him hanging around soaking it all up.

Remember that in any ad, the product is the star of the show. As the designer, your operative word is *restraint*. The shopper is not interested in your design skills; he's interested in the bike. Respect that. With however many millions of colors your printer provides, you can paint the town—but don't.

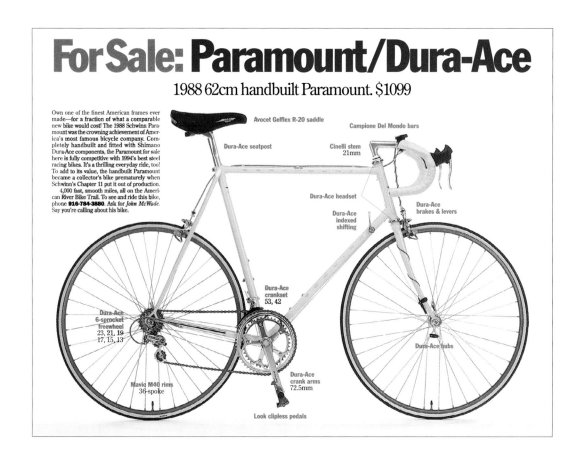

Take a color photo

The goal is to get the product as close to the buyer as we can. To do this, it must be shown in the clearest, most lifelike way. This means taking a color photo. With a product this familiar, you can simply put it on a page without background or props.

Use your judgment in staging the photo: Sometimes a prop is helpful to contextualize or explain the use of a product. For example, a teddy bear will look more inviting on a bedspread or against a pillow. Just make sure that the prop doesn't distract from or upstage the product.

White backdrop

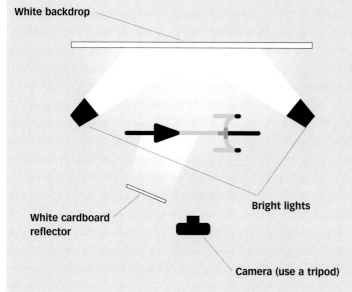

To "burn out" the background, set your product on a light floor before a clean white wall. Your lights must be very bright; if you don't have floodlights, you'll have to take the photo outdoors (set the exposure for the product, not the background). Your product will look best brightly and evenly lighted. Reflect light into shadowy spots with white cardboard (called a "fill" light). Use a photo retouching program to delete the background.

Bright lights

White cardboard reflector

Camera (use a tripod)

It's a common problem: an event to promote, an uninspiring photo, and a short deadline.

Advertising a speaker? Here's how

The best thing about a promotional design for a speaker is that it's made of simple parts. It has one picture, one message (who's saying what, when and where), and one purpose: to attract an audience.

The real fun of attending a live event is to be on the scene, to touch a celebrity, to experience *in person* what a speaker has to say. For the designer, the way to draw a crowd to your program is to capture that *you-are-there* feeling on paper.

How? It's easy: Just put the reader face to face with the speaker.

Put the speaker—not the speech, not the occasion, not anything else—center stage. Your speaker *is* the attraction; present this person *in person*, as lifelike and touchable as you can. Do this even if your speaker is not well known.

Obviously, it's crucial to have a photo of the person. Bear in mind as you examine an original photo that its context, mood and framing are immaterial (unlike a home snapshot). Look past these factors. Visualize! You're going to rescue your speaker from that little rectangular world and place her in a new setting.

What's a bloom?

No matter how compelling the topic, it takes a real person to deliver a speech, and it's a real person we go to hear. There are simply no exceptions to this, which makes it easy to design an ad. Just put everything in orbit around the speaker.

Before: The designer of this version was worried that his photo wasn't very exciting, so he reduced it to postage stamp-size and favored a title instead. Mrs. Hoke may not be known worldwide, but diminishing the speaker in favor of her speech put the caboose before the engine and left us with a confused, unappealing message. (Can you tell it's a speech?)

BEFORE

The Women's Ministry of Briarwood South presents:

Bloom Where You're Planted

How to Be Content in Difficult Circumstances

Saturday, February 1, 2002 9:30am–2:30pm

in the Briarwood Chapel
at 2200 Briarwood Way.

Cost is $5.00.
Lunch will be provided.

Martha Hoke

Registration Form

Name _____

Home phone _____

Address _____

Number of children to be placed in Nursery _____

Mail or phone registration to: **Lee Woolnough**   **995-9668**
3653 Tall Timber Dr. Birmingham 35242
Make checks payable to Briarwood South.

AFTER

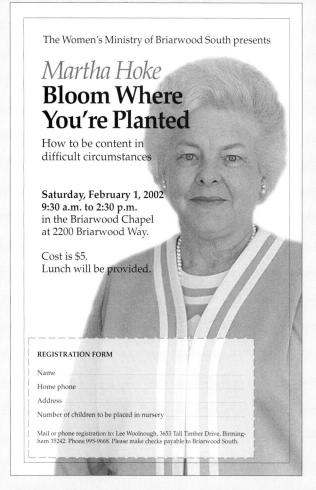

The Women's Ministry of Briarwood South presents

Martha Hoke
Bloom Where You're Planted

How to be content in difficult circumstances

Saturday, February 1, 2002
9:30 a.m. to 2:30 p.m.
in the Briarwood Chapel
at 2200 Briarwood Way.

Cost is $5.
Lunch will be provided.

REGISTRATION FORM

Name

Home phone

Address

Number of children to be placed in nursery

Mail or phone registration to: Lee Woolnough, 3653 Tall Timber Drive, Birmingham 35242. Phone 995-9668. Please make checks payable to Briarwood South.

After: The words are no different, but by elevating our speaker, the message they send has become crystal clear.

A greeting at the door

Place your photo right here like a hostess standing at the door. You can adjust the illusion somewhat by cropping from side to side. One design goal: Conceal the photo's cropped edges.

> **NOTE**
>
> Your picture will be big, so you'll need every available dot of detail. Scanner resolution should be at least double the halftone screen of your final output. For 150 lines per inch halftones, we scanned at 300 dots per inch.

How big? Think distance rather than size

You want your speaker to seem life-size

On a 5½ × 8½-inch page, how big is that? Here's a visualization technique: Think *distance* rather than size. In your mind's eye, picture yourself in a mirror, or envision a friend in a doorway. These are familiar frames, or points of reference. Then resize your subject until she seems 3 or 4 feet away. The closer you bring the reader, the closer the implied relationship. Generally speaking, closer is better.

Even if you prefer a more distant look, avoid leaving a cropped photo just floating—it spoils the illusion.

The words are easy

Since your speaker will carry the ad, there's no need for fancy type. Select one family (here, Palatino) and create hierarchy by altering size, style, shading and position.

Write on her head, but watch the details

Words and pictures can share space

It will seem funny at first, but it's totally acceptable—even desirable—to put your words right on the picture. The ad at the right is typical Madison Avenue. This technique is used with huge success on book jackets, magazine covers and in advertising of all kinds. What you'll find interesting is that it works not only for celebrities but also for regular people (really). An unfamiliar, everyday face in extreme close-up can be quite compelling.

Details make a difference

Left: The headline looks good atop the photo but does not fit: It has stranded a widow, a one-word line. A headline should not be left like this. The solution is simple.

Right: Uh-oh. The deckhead, a descriptive subtitle, fits in one line, all right, but looks like a second set of eyebrows. You'll find every situation unique; watch for similar pitfalls.

Float the form

The bottom of the page is a logical place for a form, but watch out: If you fill the space edge to edge (below left), you will box in the picture and lose that *you-are-there* feeling. The solution? Make the card smaller so that it floats in the foreground (below right). Even better: Recrop the photo beyond the border (right) and make the form translucent.

For a sense of spaciousness, extend the photo beyond the border and make the form translucent.

Type seem blah? Set better headlines with tight letterspacing and shaded letters

Big type is different from small type

The typefaces that come with your laser printer are spaced to look best at text sizes—such as 8, 9, and 10 points. At these small sizes, the reader's eye can absorb acres of words at once, because each small word blends with a gray ocean of other small words.

As type gets bigger and its spacing proportionally wider, the sweep of the eye is interrupted by now-evident lines, curves and gaps. To restore smooth reading, the letters should be kerned (letterspacing tightened); the larger the type, the tighter it should fit.

Martha Hoke
Bloom Where
You're Planted

PALATINO ROMAN 20/20, DEFAULT LETTERSPACING

Martha Hoke
Bloom Where
You're Planted

PALATINO ITALIC AND BOLD 20/18, LETTERSPACING TIGHTENED

Palatino's default spacing, which looks right at text sizes, is too airy at headline size (top); the fix is to tighten the letterspacing (bottom). Like other laser printer standards, Palatino also has little natural contrast between its roman and bold weights. An excellent way to heighten this contrast is to set the speaker's name in italics and also color it a lighter shade (here, 60 percent).

What to do if your photograph is already cropped

We had a good picture to work with; in face, Mrs. Hoke's photo is practically ideal: It's dignified, in focus, low contrast and uncropped to the waist, a real advantage.

Life isn't always so kind; often as not you'll be handed a picture that's already cropped. Now what? It is a dilemma from which even the best photo retouching software cannot extract you.

Your design goal doesn't change, however; you'll still want your speaker on stage, lifelike, touchable, nearby.

Try this:

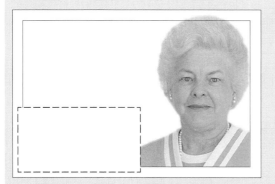

1. Conceal the cropped edges
Turn your page sideways and rule a 0.25-point border about 2 picas in, then place your photo against this border. This eliminates two of its three visible edges.

2. Break the border
Float the coupon as before, but note that in this case it "breaks the border," which smoothly conceals the third photo edge. (It also forestalls an artificial, boxed-in look.)

3. Draw a line instead of a box
We don't want that line through her head. Rather, we want our speaker to come forward as much as possible. Replace the box with 0.25-point lines, stopping at her head.

4. Now add your words.
Note the sense of depth that the various levels create.

A phone that's on the move needs a directory that can keep pace.

Small phone, smaller phone book

This pocket-sized phone book offers a simple, inexpensive way to keep your name in front of prospects. The first and last panels on side 1 are the back and front covers, and the first panel of side 2 provides space for a greeting. The remaining panels provide space for jotting down names and numbers in alphabetical order. Repeat your contact information throughout, and enter it as one of the listings. Have a commercial printer reproduce it in black and one color on 70-lb. uncoated text stock, and score and fold it accordion style.

SPECS
Single panel is 2 × 4 inches; overall 16 × 4.
Typefaces, phone book: Raleigh Gothic; subhead: Myriad Bold Condensed; Text: Myriad Condensed

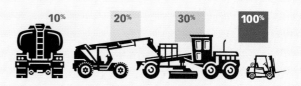

10%   20%   30%   100%

Need a quick, "custom" illustration? Layer a few
simple clip art images one over the other and
apply a different tint of the same color to each.

Flat shapes and soft grays give a 2 × 2-inch ad boldness and depth.

How to strengthen a small ad

The Kentucky Mine Summer Concert Series—
whose namesake reaches back to the Gold
Rush—is low-budget entertainment under the
stars. Volunteer townspeople pitch in to take
tickets, staff concessions, present door prizes.
Advertising this event is equally on the cheap—
a 2 × 2-inch spot all summer in the local weekly,
which itself is something of a Gold Rush relic.
Printed with black ink that could be mistaken
for tar, on cheap stock, with half the ads pasted
up by hand.

　　Problem is, small ads tend to get equally
small effort from the paper, often being tossed
together, sometimes in minutes, by an inexperienced staffer more interested in lunch.

　　But a small, simple ad can be done well in a
short time. The goal is an ad that looks good,
prints well, stands out on the page, and—
especially important—draws interest. The
key words are *keep it simple* and *be bold*.
Have a look.

It's the right idea
There's plenty of fiddling at these concerts, all right, and
the typeface—Caslon Antique—conveys the splintery,
earthy character of the Kentucky Mine, but the centered
composition is static, and the raggedy detail is too small
to make an impact.

1 Bold means simple

The first step is to simplify everything, which means *eliminate detail*. We encounter detail in the photo and in the fine, small typefaces. This violin has an excellent, descriptive shape, so in a photo manipulation program, we will replace its grays with solid black. (Open the image, clear the background, and fill the silhouette with black.)

2 Bold means big

Uncropped in the original and small enough to fit the space, the violin seems to float in mid-air, weakly. Get major. Scale it up much too large for the space, anchor it to the bottom and push it right. The eye must now move *into* the violin, while the descriptive neck sends the eye skyward. Result: We have some visual action in this space.

3 Bold means dense

Normal leading

KENTUCKY MINE

Negative leading

KENTUCKY MINE

At right, type set normally has extra leading, which is correct for text, but as a headline, it's too airy. Without ascenders or descenders, all caps can be set with negative leading; the block at right is set 25/17.5 point.

Bold means heavy

The raggedness of the original type was the right idea, but the font is too light, too full of white, and like the violin appears to float. At right, the super-heavy typeface—Block Heavy T—set in all caps and tightly compressed, squeezes the white out. Park it in the top-left corner; note how it fills the corner and radiates into the space. Action.

4 Now add depth

In solid black, every object sits on the surface conveying the same level of information. But there are four distinct thoughts here: the mine, the series, the violin and the page. By adding only two values of gray—20 percent and 60 percent—we separate all four by depth, violin in front, page in back; Kentucky Mine in dark gray gets major billing.

Note the overlap. This is a small point of interest but also tension; the two shades must always be different.

TINTS: K100, K60, K20, WHITE

5 Headline forward

Three closely spaced grays—20, 40 and 60 percent—soften the ad and recede together, so the headline in black stands forward. Visual weight is the center. What's evident now is how even the spacial volumes are. Note, below, that SUMMER CONCERT SERIES fits the spaces below and beside it almost exactly.

TINTS: K100, K60, K40, K20

6 Midrange, light

What's fun with gray is how easy it is to manipulate emphasis. Here, white headline and dark violin share the stage—a midrange background (above, 40 percent) allows both white and black elements to stand apart equally. The headline makes it obvious that white, normally regarded as a passive backdrop, is actually a color like any other. Don't forget it.

TINTS: K60, K40, K20, WHITE

7 Midrange, dark

As the field darkens beyond 50 percent, the ad—at least this one—takes on a sense of nighttime, mood, even sensuality. It's here that white begins to come forward and black recede, opposite of the original effect. The thing to remember is *edge*. The less contrast between edges, the quieter and less demanding the image.

TINTS: K80, K60, K40, WHITE

8 Black

Black has power—the more black the more power. This little ad will get noticed. When black is the primary background, however, use white judiciously. Here, the white violin has made *edge* a limiting factor. The extreme contrast overpowers the small gray type on top of it. A solution is to gray the violin, or put the type elsewhere.

7 p.m. EVERY FRIDAY
JULY 11 THROUGH AUGUST 29
KENTUCKY MINE AMPHITHEATER

TINTS: BLACK, K60, K40, WHITE

Keep in mind that any given gray looks lighter against black than against white; adjust accordingly. The "N's" here are both 50 percent gray. Cover each side and compare.

How to design versatile catalog pages that draw the reader into the action.

Create dramatic photo layouts for your products

Ever come across a really appealing catalog—one that's visually attractive, where you look at every picture, read every caption, and maybe even place an order? Notice the design? A little, probably—but that's because good design was at work; the designer succeeded in drawing your attention not to the graphics but to the *product*.

That's our challenge, too. To illustrate it, we will reexamine the design of a catalog of posters and postcards showing vintage and high-tech

aircraft. These products are unique, but the principles behind the design are not: They apply to any product catalog, a yearbook, newsletter photos of the company picnic, anywhere you're faced with a large number of similarly formatted images.

Let's focus first on structure, then on typography, the two keys to this kind of design, and show you how to create uniformity and variety on your pages at the same time.

All images available in postcards or blank greeting cards.

Cards are 5" x 7", printed on 100 lb. cover stock and laminated with polypropylene.

To Order Cards:

BEFORE

Headlines float, and low-tech typeface (Times) belies its high-tech subject.

Grounded

The designer started off right by setting up a neat, four-column grid, but then—uh-oh—filled it wall to wall with photos. This yields the most product per page but leaves the presentation static and uninviting. To sell effectively, you want to move the reader thoughtfully from one image to the next, which is done visually with scale and composition. When you fill the grid, every image hits the reader at once. The postcard motif was meant to be realistic, but borders and folders are unnaturally heavy, and the brown parchment backdrop seems the very antithesis of airy blue skies. The page heading—a key flag for the shopper—is tiny and easily overlooked, and the sprawling price format bears no relationship to that on subsequent pages.

AFTER

Room to fly

This inviting presentation is a combination of neat grid-work, fresh open space, visual variety and good typography. *Every element serves the product.* Cutout photos are exciting and draw attention instantly; note how they point like arrows inward. The page is airy. The section heading is clear but appropriately low-key; pricing information is sleek and uniform.

Since every product on this page is a postcard, showing the format 46 times is repetitive. Just show it once and leave the remaining photos unencumbered.

Helicopter for hire

What an impact a super-size cutout makes—it thrusts the reader dramatically into the action! A cutout like this works on any page, whether your product is airplanes, jewelry or a video. Why? It gives your layout a point of entry, a way in. It's important, then, to provide subsequent stepping stones—usually more cutouts—to which the reader can easily jump. This sequential *first here, then there, then over there*, keeps the reader's eye moving and the visual interest high. By arranging cutouts around the perime-

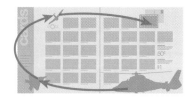

ter facing inward, the reader makes a loop around the main group of photos. If you also keep text to the outside, the reader will rapidly take in every key piece of your information.

These spaces roughly equal

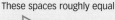

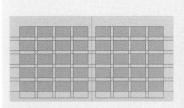 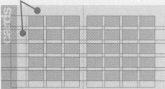 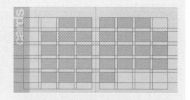

a. Block out a grid
Photos want all the empty space you can give them. Set up w-i-d-e page margins—6 picas at least, 2 between columns—then divide the area into equal blocks matching the proportions of your photos.

b. Delete the first column
Delete a full column, then create a column-width section head and push it to the far-left edge. This isn't common to all designs; most heads are on top. The idea is to loosen the page with an empty buffer.

c. Remove a few perimeter blocks
Remove a few blocks from around the edges. Here you're making the grid less block-like by giving it an irregular edge and freeing up spaces to place cutout photos. Note the asymmetry.

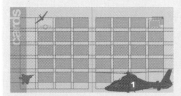  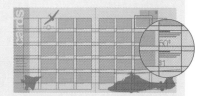

d. Create a focal point
Cutout photos are exciting. Select several, delete backgrounds, then place their irregular forms where blocks once were. Scale one up really, really big. Point images inward, as close to the group as you can.

e. Create a hierarchy of sizes
Now enlarge the remaining cutouts to a variety of smaller sizes. The descending scale that results will lead the reader fluidly around the layout, taking in the cutouts before proceeding to the main group.

f. Add text outside the cluster
Fit text into empty grid squares, aligned to the top and left edges, always to the outside of the main group. This adds to the artful irregularity of the edge and establishes a uniform, easy-to-read style.

A well-managed variety of rectangles

Turn the page and our catalog is now selling posters, which are physically much larger than postcards. We want to signify the difference, so the four-column grid has been changed to three. This, however, yields fewer places to delete blocks, so it's time for two more variety-making techniques: Merge blocks, then enter the empty airspace.

BEFORE

AFTER

A balanced layout

When arranging your page, you want your layout's center of gravity to be near its center. Bear in mind that while photos have "weight," so does empty space. Factors affecting weight are size, value (dark-light) and distance from center. Examples here are all well balanced.

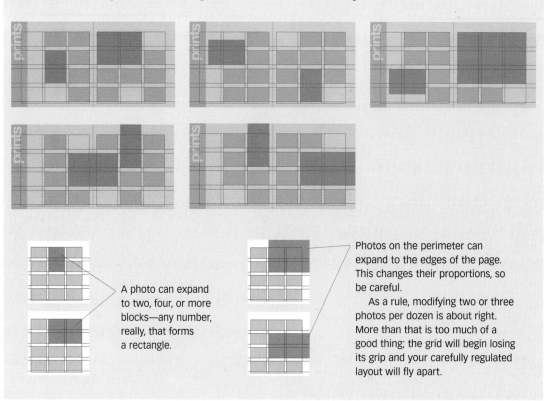

A photo can expand to two, four, or more blocks—any number, really, that forms a rectangle.

Photos on the perimeter can expand to the edges of the page. This changes their proportions, so be careful.

As a rule, modifying two or three photos per dozen is about right. More than that is too much of a good thing; the grid will begin losing its grip and your carefully regulated layout will fly apart.

There can be only one dominant object

Every spread must have one focal point. This is usually the biggest image, sometimes the brightest. The dominant photo may be rectangular or cut out, near the center or on the perimeter (usually better), but like the star of any show there can be only one (right)—all others must be smaller. Two photos with equal pull (below) will weaken your design.

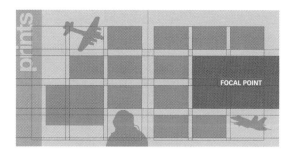

FOCAL POINT

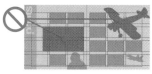

This spread has battling focal points. Pick one dominant object and let it rule.

Overlaps add depth

A fun-to-apply technique is to lap a cutout photo into an adjacent space or onto another photo. This imparts a three-dimensional quality that practically lifts the image off the page! Equally important, it creates a visual bridge that draws the eye from one area to the next and keeps the reader moving around the layout. An overlapped photo has other uses; it can soften hard edges and make apparently unrelated material appear related.

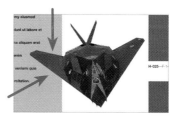

The grid is for captions, too

If your layout includes brief captions, they go inside the grid blocks as shown—you'll have to plan ahead for this. Don't shoehorn them between blocks afterward. The space below captions should be the same as the space between photos, never less. To look best, all captions should be the same number of lines; if they're not, the longest should be your yardstick. Paragraph-length captions look best not beneath photos at all but set into the grid in whole blocks; two or three can share one block.

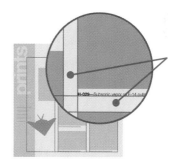

Watch for trapped space

As you're arranging your layout, avoid trapping empty space—that is, surrounding it on all sides. Empty space should always have an open path to the outside of your layout. A cutout centered in a block traps space above it. The solution is to push it as close to the group as you can. Bottom right, cutout photos sometimes trap space no matter how close they are. You may have to live with it, but if you have a caption or callout, this where to put it.

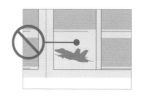

Empty space is trapped.

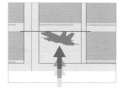

Align the cutout with tops of adjacent blocks.

Empty space can be a good place for callouts or captions.

Like many catalogs, *Mach 1* also has an editorial section; in this issue, it's promoting a new book. It's an exciting book, too, with an exotic topic and truly excellent photographs. We want to convey this excitement to the reader, and for this the grid provides an outstanding framework.

BEFORE

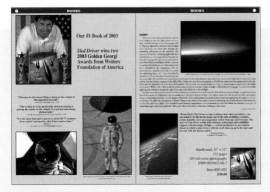

Page without a plan
Oops. Even the best photos fade if they're displayed like items in a garage sale. By consigning the photos to the perimeter of the layout and leaving them without a focal point, contrasts or any visible relationship or structure, the designer of this spread completely dissipated their potency.

AFTER

A fast-moving layout has a strong visual center
Here are the techniques we've learned so far: Note the huge focal point. Around it in a tight hierarchy are five supporting images, including for contrast a cutout of the pilot-author. The cutout makes the most of his irregular, organic form, which contrasts sharply with the hard-edged, mechanical lines of the aircraft. A second cutout on the far left bridges two visual areas and points inward. All text and empty space stays outside the photo group.

Group related elements

When assembling a collection of diverse elements like this—section head, lead, headline, article, quotations, photos and so on—it may help to think of your layout as a fine table setting, and group related elements—plates here, silverware there, glassware on top. For this layout, we have already established a location on the far left for the section head. Because the reader naturally moves left to right, note here the editorial and quotations (1 & 2) come next, followed by the cluster of photos (3). While for photos you have the option of fitting grid blocks exactly or expanding them outward, the rule for text is less flexible: Text should fit the grid. Here the editorial fills single columns; the quotations span two.

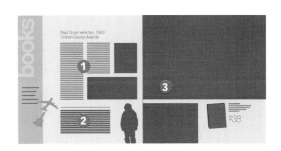

Create a visual axis

The strongest way to hold together a tight cluster of photos is to create a visual axis near the center of your layout. The main body of photos revolve around this axis. Note the axis also serves as a point of alignment for, in this case, the bottom of the editorial, as well as the book cover and price information. Result: a well-organized layout with a strong visual center that keeps the reader moving fluidly around the page.

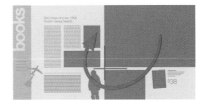

A word about relative scale
Does your layout feature different-size objects? Jump from three columns to four, or four columns to five, or whatever—but not on the same spread. Other dimensions (margins, space between columns, etc.) and type sizes must not change.

You don't sell helicopters?
That's OK—the principles behind this design—an underlying grid, a single type family—and visual details like overlapping photos can be applied to any layout.

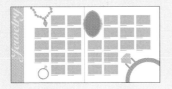

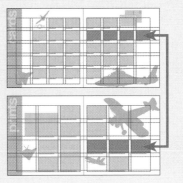

Select a single type family

In a photographic layout such as this one, *the photos are the show*—and type is a supporting player. The type must therefore complement the graphics—even heighten their effect—but stay out of the limelight. The most efficient way to do this is to use a single type family, one preferably with three or more weights. Each weight must then be applied consistently. For example, all subheads might be in bold, all prices in light, and so on. A change in weight signals the reader that the information is different.

Different weights of Helvetica Neue are used.

Skilled use of contrasts gets the most from your type choice

Value, or dark-light contrast, is a powerful design tool, illustrated here by a section head. At such a large size (left), white on black (right) would be overpowering. White on light blue is softer; very low-contrast blues yield the subtlety we want. By its prominent size, the word says, "heading," but by its low contrast imparts its information quietly, in proportion to its worth.

Size and weight are contrasts that can be used to balance each other. Here, the price is very large but *very light*, and thereby draws the reader's eye but doesn't dominate its neighbors.

Important recurring elements such as this price block must look the same from page to page. In our case, it's aligned left and fit to the top-left corner of a grid block. Note the confidently small *Postcards* heading. Can we get away with this? Sure! Because price and position have drawn your eye. Look again at the previous spreads.

Stationery

The first step toward great stationery is to build a solid foundation.

How to lay out a stationery system

Good stationery is much more than just a logo on paper. In fact, very handsome stationery may have no logo at all. Beneath the surface is a "system" by which each piece relates to the others in an orderly way—when seen together, the letterhead, envelope and business card appear as family members; taken alone, each makes an intelligent statement.

A system approach will quickly bring order and style to your designs. It has other advan-

tages, too: Its orderliness is easy to live with for a long time, and a system adapts readily to a wide range of uses. The basic package may later be expanded to include fax covers, invoices, memo sheets, brochures and other common documents.

The chief goal of system design is to *promote consistency*. To realize this, we retain the same logo size, type size, type composition and margins throughout.

Create some axes and intersections by marking off spaces reserved for letter writing, postal requirements and margins—spaces that cannot vary much. These are the intersections in which we are interested.

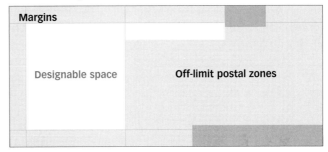

Business card
3½ × 2 inches

Margins

Designable space

No. 10 envelope 9½ × 4⅛-inches

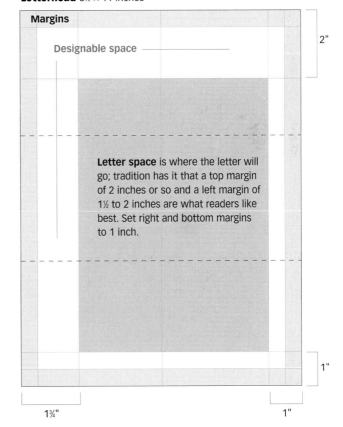

Margins

Designable space   **Off-limit postal zones**

Postal space is the acreage the post office wants. For Business Reply Mail and other uses, the space required can be quite extensive. (The post office or its Web site can supply you with documents that contain exact specs.) To be safe, stick to the left one-third of the envelope; that way, you can accommodate postal data in the future without a redesign.

Letterhead 8½ × 11 inches

Half-inch margins not only guide your design but also allow for printing on even a very small press by providing room for the "grippers"—the mechanical fingers that grip the paper and pull it through the rollers. Set a half-inch margin around letterhead and envelope, and a quarter-inch around your business card. (Business cards are normally printed eight or more to the sheet—with margin room to spare—and therefore need no gripper room.) Envelopes require gripper room on any press unless the envelopes are to be "manufactured," which means they're first printed on flat paper and assembled afterward by machine, a technique that allows for bleeds and embossing.

Margins

Designable space

2"

Letter space is where the letter will go; tradition has it that a top margin of 2 inches or so and a left margin of 1½ to 2 inches are what readers like best. Set right and bottom margins to 1 inch.

1"

1¾"   1"

For best results, type should be used with restraint. Pay attention to these factors:

What size?

Type will be the same size on all three pieces: letterhead, envelope and business card. Therefore, the type (and graphics) must be proportioned to the business card because it is the smallest piece. For this, 7-, 8- or 9-point type is ideal; 10-point is too big.

Make only one typographic contrast, which may mean size *or* style *or* color *or* weight *or* italics. For example:

Skipjack's Fish Market
3467 Ocean Beach
Fort Bragg
California 95437

…sends one typographic signal. And:

Skipjack's Fish Market
3467 Ocean Beach
Fort Bragg
California 95437

…sends two. Stop there; if you add more, you'll weaken the message, as in:

Skipjack's Fish Market
3467 Ocean Beach
Fort Bragg
California 95437

Each time you vary the type, you alert the reader that something has changed or is somehow different. Think of this as tugging on the reader's shirttail: Once draws the reader's attention, but twice is annoying.

What leading?

Type is customarily set with 1 or 2 points of extra leading—for example, 8/9-point. More leading, however, can be effective—it makes the reader linger momentarily to absorb the information. Below, Franklin Gothic 8/12:

Skipjack's Fish Market
3467 Ocean Beach
Fort Bragg
California 95437

What typestyles?

For most business stationery, the best type-styles are the low-key classics, the ones, ironically, that are least likely to stand out on a page of type specimens. The following 10 are suitable anywhere:

Bodoni	Bookman	Caslon
Century	Garamond	Goudy
Helvetica	Palatino	Times
Univers		

Some type families have a great deal of contrast between their various weights. For example:

Bookman Light   Helvetica Light

Bookman Bold   **Helvetica Black**

These are ideal choices when contrast is important, as in this example:

Skipjack's Fish Market
3467 Ocean Beach
Fort Bragg
California 95437

But other type has almost no contrast in weight:

Palatino   Times

Palatino Bold   **Times Bold**

...and so is less suitable in the same setting.

Skipjack's Fish Market
3467 Ocean Beach
Fort Bragg
California 95437

If you're limited to fonts like this, you have two good options. The first is to create a look with no contrasts at all. For example, in Garamond:

Skipjack's Fish Market
3467 Ocean Beach
Fort Bragg
California 95437

This may be scary because it's so plain, but on the page, it communicates a self-assured sense of restraint. The second option is to add another, more decorative typeface as a contrasting typographic signal. Here is about as radical as we want to get:

𝕾𝖐𝖎𝖕𝖏𝖆𝖈𝖐'𝖘 𝕱𝖎𝖘𝖍 𝕸𝖆𝖗𝖐𝖊𝖙
3467 Ocean Beach
Fort Bragg
California 95437

Remember, use one typographic contrast only—do not vary both the typestyle and type size:

𝕾𝖐𝖎𝖕𝖏𝖆𝖈𝖐'𝖘 𝕱𝖎𝖘𝖍 𝕸𝖆𝖗𝖐𝖊𝖙
3467 Ocean Beach
Fort Bragg
California 95437

While it looks OK here, this treatment draws the eye to the type, which we don't want; rather, our goal is to convey an *overall image* of a confident, well-run business. This is the function of the entire stationery system; one piece of type won't do it (exception: if the type itself is the logo).

System 1

Vertical spread to letterhead fold
- Type align left

Place your type in the upper-left corner and position the logo vertically beneath it at either of the two letterhead folds.

Note the logo is a marker for the start of the letter. This is great: It's handsome, convenient—and the reader is lured to your logo by his or her own name. Sublime.

Neither logo nor text should be placed on a fold. You don't want your company to have a crease in it. This is easy to overlook because the folds are invisible. Don't forget.

System 2

Horizontal spread to right margin

- Type align right

Place your logo in the upper-left corner; move horizontally and "hang" the type on the right margin. On the envelope, the right "margin" is an arbitrary point short of the postal zone.

Note how the logo aligns with the left letter margin.

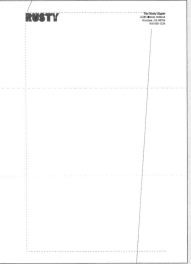

Although this logo is formed from the company name, the company name is nevertheless included in the text block.

Do not vary the size of the logo from envelope to letterhead to business card. Why? Because a reader does not "read" empty space: He or she absorbs only your mark. Quietly impress upon the reader the same clean image once, twice, three times, taking advantage of consistency and the proven power of repetition.

System 3

In-margin vertical spread
- Bleed logo
- Type centered

Align the logo with the left margin; bleed to the top edge. Position the type vertically beneath the logo at the bottom margin *or* at either of the two letterhead folds.

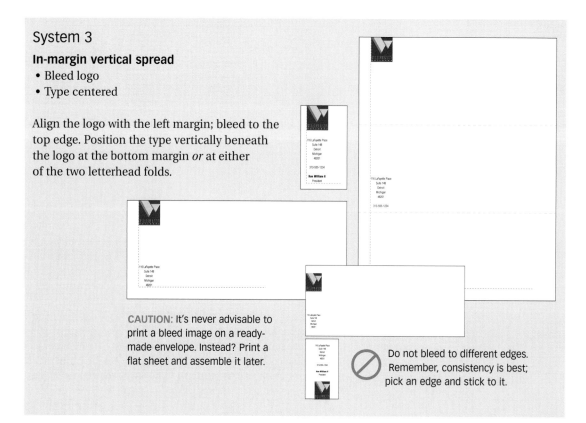

CAUTION: It's never advisable to print a bleed image on a ready-made envelope. Instead? Print a flat sheet and assemble it later.

Do not bleed to different edges. Remember, consistency is best; pick an edge and stick to it.

Fun with borders

One of the more interesting functions of a border is to *rescale* a visual field, which makes it appear to be a different size or shape than it is naturally. This treatment can be quite pretty; it can also be used to focus (or divert) a reader's attention.

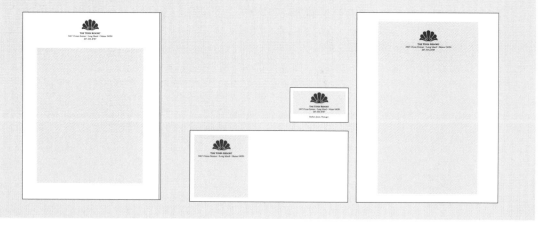

System 4

Pin register
- No variation in "signature"
- Type centered

Center your logo on the top margin; center the type directly beneath it. Note the objects are "registered"—that is, their relative positions do not change.

Here's a case where artistic license is called for: Note that the long address line forces the logo far to the right. Solution? Don't reset the type—readers will notice (because they are reading it). Instead, slip left across the grid, a move that will be invisible because the grid is invisible. This works only with pin register; don't do it if the logo or type aligns with something else on the page.

Do not vary the relationship of the logo and type: Key to the pin register system is military uniformity. (The term "pin register" is derived from a film alignment system in which two or more overlays are punched with identical holes and pressed over stubby metal pegs or "pins," ensuring that their positions do not shift.)

System 5

Vertical spread to bottom margin
• Type align left

Place your logo in the upper-left corner.
Position the type vertically beneath the logo
at the bottom margin.

More tips for success…

• Does someone in the office still use a typewriter? Design for that! Roll your laser proof
into the typewriter and type something on it.
Is everything positioned suitably? If not, feel
free to adjust the grid—it's not cast in
cement. Just be consistent.

• Don't forget to include fax numbers, e-mail
addresses, Web site addresses and so on.
• An envelope rarely carries phone and fax
numbers; be sure to delete them.
• Make sure your paper and ink colors photo-
copy clearly; test both prior to printing.

Business card plus

Your business card can be turned into a real gift for recipients, if you ask it to do just a little bit more. Here's a simple way to add function to the form.

For example, a bike shop proprietor might incorporate a metric conversion table (right). A guitar teacher could include chord diagrams (below right). A village board member can provide a list of local help-line phone numbers (below left).

For your version, use information specific to your field of interest—something that reminds recipients of your area of expertise each time he or she uses it: a list, a conversion chart, measurements, industry terminology and so on.

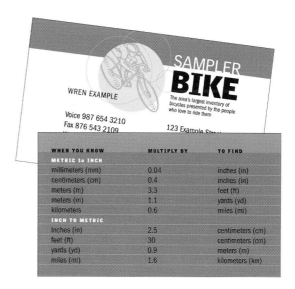

WHEN YOU KNOW	MULTIPLY BY	TO FIND
METRIC to INCH		
millimeters (mm)	0.04	inches (in)
centimeters (cm)	0.4	inches (in)
meters (m)	3.3	feet (ft)
meters (m)	1.1	yards (yd)
kilometers	0.6	miles (mi)
INCH to METRIC		
inches (in)	2.5	centimeters (cm)
feet (ft)	30	centimeters (cm)
yards (yd)	0.9	meters (m)
miles (mi)	1.6	kilometers (km)

It's more than a card; it's *you!* Here's how to look your best.

How to design a "cold call" postcard

What could be more nerve-wracking than a cold sales call? Yet what job in business is more necessary? Since without new clients no business can grow, sooner or later we must make friends with strangers.

Imagine two real estate agents working in a crowded market who have decided to cold call by mail. This is less stressful than face-to-face encounters, but at a price. It means entrusting that oh-so-important first encounter not to handshakes and a friendly voice but to a piece of paper. It had better be good.

Their first effort has all the markings of most direct mail today: too much information in too small of a space. No focal point. No main message. Let's look at how this mailer can attain an air of competence and professionalism through design.

Our world is so busy that one mailing is never enough; you'll have more success with a series of periodic mailings designed in a style the reader comes to recognize. To do this, select standards of size, color, and typography, and stick with them. It will help to design several cards before mailing any; that way you can troubleshoot any variables that crop up. The makeovers in this article are good examples of cards in a series.

Card size: 5½ × 8½ inches; **colors:** black and white (or black on colored stock); **sans serif text:** Franklin Gothic Book, italic and heavy; **serif type:** Caxton Light.

TOOMUCHALLATONCE The real estate agents had a lot of points to make, so the designer of this card tried to organize all of their information by changes in typestyle—**bold** headline, *italic* body, ***bold italic*** names, *CAP ITALICS* exclamations and so on—in blocks all evenly sized, centered and flanked by two photos. It was a good idea—typographic contrasts allow many ideas to coexist in a type space—that faltered in its execution. The problem? Its contrasts are indistinct and the material too uniformly distributed, which results in a kind of visual slurry.

To impart information fast, first sort it into a few batches of like kind—head, body and closing, for example—then separate them clearly. (The operative word here is *few*: Too many differences will hinder rather than help.) To illustrate (left), we've reduced the buzzy *Before* to four distinct blocks on a stage of clean white space. It's already easier to read. Why? Note there are fewer contrasts than before—fewer visual differences in size (big-small), weight (heavy-light), value (dark-light) and so forth— but they're much greater! The now striking differences reduce the previous mass of information to reader-friendly clumps that can be absorbed quickly and easily.

Turn your headline into a showpiece

Beautiful, eye-arresting typography will engage even the most resolute nonreader. Scale words up, up, up, crisply aligned to the left or right, then reset one in a highly contrasting typeface—here, a light serif contrasts sharply with a bold sans serif (**1**). Reduce the *bolder* word to half (or so) the other's width, lighten its value, nudge it upward until the words interact, then darken the whole backdrop. You'll find many possibilities of your own, but as you work keep an eye out for points of alignment; note that while headlines are aligned right, the remainder of the material aligns left on an invisible vertical line created by the lower word (**2**).

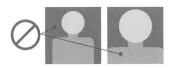

By playing with type choice, boldness and size (left), a very dynamic contrast can be acheived (above).

Scale heads the same

Mug shots are the same kind of visual information, so they should look alike. Scale all to one head size (align eyes and chins), then crop to one frame size. Here, the nonstandard squarish format that results adds a point of visual interest. Note, top, how overlapping placement draws the two visual fields together.

Set your product center stage!

Divide vertical space into horizontal segments: the photo occupies the center; text sits in the other two. Turning white space black (1) is simple and brilliant: It presents the headline with crystal clarity and is especially versatile in a series of mailers that rely on typestyle for their identity. Why? Because any typestyle will work! Note that the bottom segment divides vertically; mug shots stand between text and names, allowing the reader to take in each in turn.

Stacked mug shots (2) team with a photo to form a natural sight line. This is a bonus to watch for that you won't always find. As a rule, keep the visual weight centered or rightward. An overlapping mug (3) draws the two visual fields together. The overlap just flirts; too much and the mug will "hook up" with the photo above it.

Name-title text blocks (4) illustrate the correct use of bold-light-italic contrasts; changes are small and each signals a different kind of information.

Larger home? Smaller home? Investment property? Whether you're buying or selling, put two real estate professionals on your team. List with us today, start packing tomorrow!

Mike Ognissanti
Ryland Mortgage
Financing Expert
484-0255

Edgar Cordell
/Better Homes Realty
Marketing Professional
966-4101

4 Use type contrast to signify different types of information.

1

2

3

Ghostbuster
When *communication* is paramount, the cleaner the design the better. If you desire the patina of a ghosted background photo, your foreground must be clean as a whistle. Here, small text blocks and crisp left alignment let the photo *show*.

Illustrate an idea

Clip art is inexpensive and bold—solid black reproduces anywhere—and often works when text and photos do not (a photo might be too literal, text insufficiently picturesque). Silhouettes take advantage of the power of suggestion. Extended hands (**1**) suggest a meeting yet to come, teamwork and so on; the giant SOLD (**2**) suggests the result you'd hope for. Composition is important; note in each case the visual weight is in the center.

Self-framing layout
A bold horizon line anchors the layout; light elbow lines direct the eye. Key, though, is that all abut invisible margins (left). Don't forget.

Reverse scale
An unexpected technique turns the table on reality, providing a visual surprise—and, of course, the suggestion that buyer and seller, not the house, control the transaction. Only clip art can pull this off.

Make an instant invitation

Need an 11th-hour card or invitation? Here's a civilized idea that's easy to print on an in-office printer: Make this letter-size template—it folds neatly into a standard envelope (ask for a 5½ Baronial), and save it to craft personal sentiments on a moment's notice.

Set up the page...
Letter size, landscape mode, single-sided, Margins: 2 picas (or so). Number of columns: 2, 4 picas between (double the margin width).

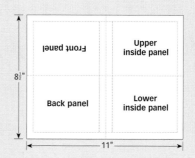

Add your creative touches...
Note the front panel is upside down. Before you begin, make sure your chosen layout program can rotate both text and graphics.

Print. Then fold once...

Twice..

And deliver it proudly.

Introduce yourself while engaging your prospect with this charming design.

A business card brochure is a mini-marketer

What could be more efficient—or intriguing? A seemingly common business card folds out into a handsome, quick-reading brochure, then tears off for convenient filing. Its originality and brevity will leave your prospect impressed— and it's convenient, too. Handing out your card is now an occasion.

It's designed like a standard six-panel brochure—only small. The outer panel makes an introduction, then opens to reveal your company's story.

Two panels are standard 3½ × 2-inch business-card size; the flap panel is one-sixteenth-inch narrower for easy folding. Have your card printed on conventional business card stock with a perforation between the panels and business card.

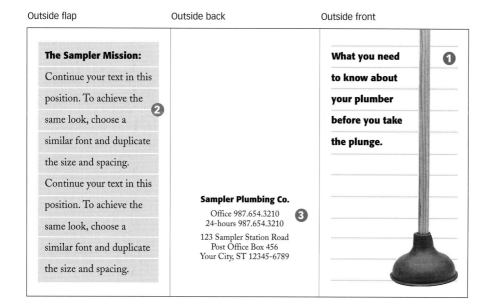

Outside flap | Outside back | Outside front

The Sampler Mission:

Continue your text in this position. To achieve the same look, choose a similar font and duplicate the size and spacing. Continue your text in this position. To achieve the same look, choose a similar font and duplicate the size and spacing.

Sampler Plumbing Co.
Office 987.654.3210
24-hours 987.654.3210

123 Sampler Station Road
Post Office Box 456
Your City, ST 12345-6789

What you need to know about your plumber before you take the plunge.

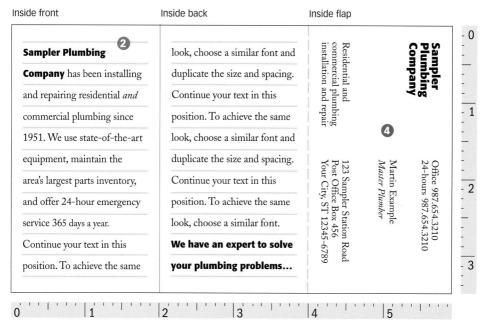

Inside front | Inside back | Inside flap

Sampler Plumbing Company has been installing and repairing residential *and* commercial plumbing since 1951. We use state-of-the-art equipment, maintain the area's largest parts inventory, and offer 24-hour emergency service 365 days a year. Continue your text in this position. To achieve the same

look, choose a similar font and duplicate the size and spacing. Continue your text in this position. To achieve the same look, choose a similar font and duplicate the size and spacing. Continue your text in this position. To achieve the same look, choose a similar font. **We have an expert to solve your plumbing problems...**

Residential and commercial plumbing installation and repair

123 Sampler Station Road
Post Office Box 456
Your City, ST 12345-6789

Sampler Plumbing Company

Martin Example
Master Plumber

Office 987.654.3210
24-hours 987.654.3210

Business card brochure
1 Headline: Formata Bold, 9/20-pt., align left; **Lines:** .5 pt.; **Tint:** 30 percent black; **2 Headline:** Formata Bold, 9/20-pt., align left; **Body text:** Caslon Regular 10/20-pt., align left; **Lines:** 0.5-pt., reverse; **Box:** 20 percent black; **3 Company name:** Formata Bold, 8/9-pt., align center; **Phone and address:** Caslon Regular 8/9-pt., align center; **4 Business card, Headline:** Formata Bold, 11/11-pt., align left; **Text:** Caslon Regular 9/10-pt., align left; **Dotted line:** 0.5-pt., 30 percent black

Design a handsome business card in this surprising space.

The invisible square

There's a lot riding on your business card. And what a challenge it is to design! It's a tiny space of fixed proportions that carries some important information (company name), some uninteresting information (fax number) that must be clearly visible (your name) and easily accessible (your phone number), all while making a

good visual impression. This means it must be organized simply and presented boldly. You'll love this format—it's so versatile. It's built on an invisible square; you put your text on *that* side in a single, neat column, and your image on *this* side, and let it do the talking. It's flexible and fun.

The U.S. standard business card is 3½ × 2-inches, horizontal format.

Measure in 2 inches, set your type, and look at what results: a lovely white square. This is your stage.

In practice, the type will be ragged, like this. The key is to have a strong vertical edge. To do this, set one topic per line—name on one line, title on the next, phone on the third, and so on.

You can flip the layout. If you do this, the text must now align right—somewhat slower to read—to maintain the edge.

How could anyone resist? If you have a good photo, you can't present yourself with more impact than this. It's engaging, entertaining and clear as a bell. A background distracts more often than not, so as a rule, just get rid of it. Emphasize one text point by using a distinctive type size and weight.

Typefaces
Dog trainer: Flyer Black Condensed; **All else:** Frutiger Light Condensed

Sandy Williams

DOG TRAINER

757-891-5487 cell
757-624-6383 phone
2280 Hekin Terrace Way
Norfolk, VA 23504
dogtrainer@attbi.com
www.sandythetrainer.com

Where do the important words go? Along important lines in the picture; here Sandy's DOG TRAINER title matches her dog's eyes in size, weight and color.

Less obvious is the gap beneath the title, but it's the same as the gap between eyes and nose. You'll never see this consciously. But it's why the spacing looks right.

If your subject lends itself to a series, why not have more than one card? It's fun for you and customers, too. Use the same information on all.

Typeface
Glypha Roman and Black

Hey, what works for our pets will work for us. If you're comfortable in front of a camera, this is an extremely appealing way to make an impression, leave an impression, and jog a memory. A smiling face is so real, so personal, there's no way you'll turn into just another number. To really connect, smile straight into the camera. An above-it-all, off-in-the-distance portrait pose will totally defeat the effect. A common mistake is to retain a background, which makes the photo look like an ordinary snapshot. Pure white has unusual clarity and leaves all of the attention on you.

Very low key, the text is set in a single size of a single face; his name and company name are set apart only by bold type. The entire text block is light gray (60 percent). Subtle and handsome. The quieter the type, the more attention the photo gets.

Note that his shoulder laps across the vertical edge; this looks more natural than artificially scissoring it off, and it keeps his face centered in the square. It's a detail, but pay attention; stuff like this can mysteriously mess up an otherwise good design.

3 | Full-page photo

Typefaces
Yasha's: Sloop Script One; **Text:** Bembo

Photos with very quiet backgrounds can be left intact; in this case, the radiant light of the background adds an appealing depth. This is a staged shot dramatically cropped; the idea was to find the *least* amount of image that would convey the *most* information. When looking for an image like this, think *theater*—the visual suggestion of person, place, business, whatever, has dramatic impact that is often more appealing than coldly seeing it.

Yasha's focal point is a beautiful script that corresponds in size, position and color to the red cherry. Picking a matching color is easy; just eyedropper it out of the photo. Note the orange glass is centered in the invisible square; the swashy "Y" crosses the vertical edge.

4 | The no-longer invisible square

Typefaces
Ralena: Hairspray Brunette; **Text:** Futura Book and Bold

This whimsical appointment card makes the square visible, and in doing so, makes the white rectangle visible, too. Because both sides are now clearly defined, it is no longer necessary for the text to maintain the edge. Note that

"Hair design by…" offsets Ralena's curlicue signature, a composition not possible on the other cards.

This beautiful image is visually opposite Example 3 on the previous page. The background is similarly quiet, full of radiant light, but it's all dark. The beautiful solution: Just reverse the type. The text draws attention to both store name and manager, yet keeps the visual hierarchy intact. To do this, two techniques are involved: BAJA TROPICALS set in a large, stylish typeface conveys the image, while the manager's name is the plain text face set in bold caps.

Typefaces
Baja Tropicals: Lithos Regular; **Text:** Franklin Gothic Condensed and Book Condensed

The full-page image easily masks the fact that we're working with a square, but it's still here. Note the fish—almost square, too—is framed fairly evenly in the space.

Why is the name down here? Because those kissy lips are pointing right toward it. Actually, the whole fish is pointing down here; watch for similar lines of sight. What's great is that the reader never notices; your name just silently gets attention.

The primary text focal point corresponds to the primary visual focal point.

White on black is severe, powerful and always gets attention. In addition to its popular, high-tech look, this minimalist design has another advantage: It's as cheap as ordinary black and white.

Typefaces
Avenir Light and Black

Set type all caps, all one size, slightly S-P-A-C-E-D, then pull the name across the invisible square (left). Note DRAKE remains aligned. Gray the type (here, 30 percent) so that the name in white stands out.

The black-red-white combination is handsome, aggressive and almost literally arresting. With red as the middle value, black and white words have the most contrast and depth. More raw power for the buck than any other two colors.

It looks at a glance like illustration may be involved, but this handsome logo consists only of letters atop a square. Its visual complexity, however—the fancy typeface, the square, the name, the title, big type, small type, uppercase, lowercase, and so on—gave us some compositional problems to solve.

Typeface
Nuptial Script

Center the entire logo in the square. Evident even without the dashed line, note the square "air" framing the image.

Small adjustments in size and spacing align the text. The large white "S" above the line is OK; its visual weight is trivial.

Name and logo are connected visually, yet both are set apart. Karen's name is larger than its adjacent text, but in recessive white it draws attention quietly.

Here's a useful way to stretch your photo library. "Transitional living for homeless families with children" suggests a family-type picture, but the happy gang here is too, well, *not* homeless. The solution? Cast them in silhouette.

Typeface
Head and info: Khaki Two; **Subtitle:** Century Expanded Italic

Informal typeface lightens a serious subject. As a counterpoint, note the bulk of the text aligns with the bulk of the image, putting the center of gravity firmly on the bottom and silently conveying *stability*.

Black, white and gray yield three levels of visual depth: recessive white in back, black in front, gray between. This is a sophisticated way to distinguish one line from the next without adding complexity by changing typeface, style or size.

Business Documents

Versatile and economical, this design can contain all of the materials you need to impress customers.

Create a do-it-all business portfolio

Here's an easy, attractive corporate portfolio you can re-create for yourself. It's a complete system made up of elements that you can mix and match for any business opportunity.

The **portfolio cover** is the container—it holds all of the other elements for a presentation or mailing, and has diecuts to hold the business card and brochure. The **brochure** is sized to fit in the business envelope, in case you want to send it out by itself. It has a flap in back where you can tuck in a letter or a price list, and a slot to hold the business card, so the brochure really can stand alone. A series of color-coordinated **direct-mail postcards** can be planned and printed up at the same time the package is produced—to save on printing costs—then mailed out later at intervals.

Finally, the **stationery** package is tied in with the overall scheme via color as well as function. The business envelope does double duty as a carrier for both the letterhead and the

brochure, and the business card can travel along in the diecuts in either the brochure or portfolio cover. When you want to mail the portfolio, the matching mailing label turns any standard white catalog envelope into a coordinated element of the system—and also comes in handy when you mail out odd-size packages.

This system is a designer's dream, a great example of *less is more*. Just a few colors give the look of a rich color scheme. One font used in several sizes and widths gives an illusion of variety; and a few print pieces add up to a package that delivers a lot of *punch*.

What more could you want? It's *easy to do*: The principles that make this package work are general enough to apply to other pieces. It's *economical*: Planning ahead, using just two or three colors, and gang printing saves money. Finally, it's *effective*: Once you've set up the logo and signature layout, you use it over and over again! Here's how to make it.

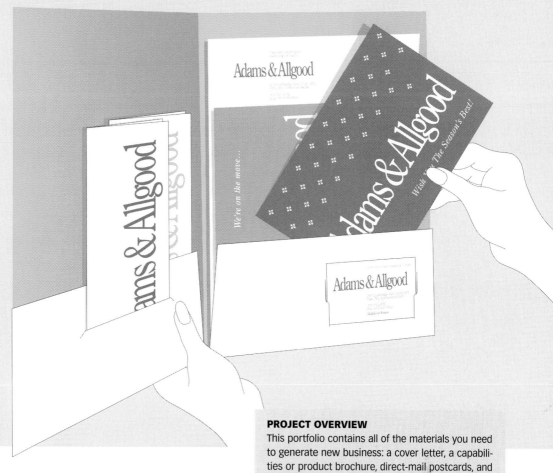

PROJECT OVERVIEW

This portfolio contains all of the materials you need to generate new business: a cover letter, a capabilities or product brochure, direct-mail postcards, and your business card. It's loaded with unique features that make it easy to work with, inexpensive to print and endlessly versatile.

A simple one-font type system

A single, medium-weight font yields a variety of easy good looks.

A simple three-color scheme

Color on white, and white knocked out of solid color swatches make this color scheme look more expensive than it really is.

A simple, elegant use of space

White space is the surest, cheapest way to achieve a look of quality, and that translates to a stable, professional image.

TALK TO YOUR PRINTER

This is one project where it will really pay to contact your printer at the very beginning. It will take a pro to recommend the best use of paper and color, and to lay out the press sheet to get the maximum number of pieces on it. Try to plan so that you print two colors on one side—and just one color on the other side—of the press sheet.

Introducing the system of elements

It's a designer's dream: one typestyle simply and uniformly applied; three pretty colors that look like more. Mix and match—even add new pieces easily—for any occasion.

The portfolio cover

Measurements: Each cover panel measures 9 inches wide and 12 inches tall; the flaps measure 4 inches deep and taper in to 3 picas wide. The diecut for the business card should be 0p3 wider than the business card at the widest point, and 4p *narrower* at the narrowest point. Its height should *equal* that of the business card. The diecut for the brochure should be 3p wider than the width of the brochure, with a 1p6-long 45-degree taper at each end.

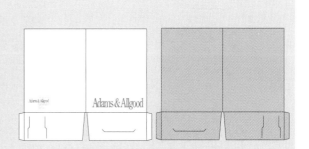

Paper: Use heavy cover stock (about 80 lb.) for the portfolio and brochure covers, the postcards and the business card, then gang them on the same press sheet.

The brochure cover

Measurements: Each cover panel measures 4 inches wide and 9 inches tall. The bottom flap measures 18p deep, is centered on the bottom of the back panel, is 22p6 wide at the fold, and tapers in to 19p6 at the tip. The side flap measures 23p wide, and tapers from a height of 30p at the fold to 28p at the outside edge. The business card diecut specs are the same as on the side flap. The inside pages measure just 0p3 less than the height and width of the covers.

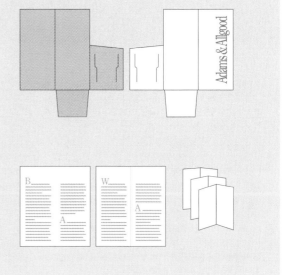

...and insides

Paper: Select a lighter weight of the same stock (about 100 lb. text) for the inside pages.

The direct-mail postcards

Measurements: The postcards can be any size you wish and could even be sized to fit into any odd leftover space you may have on a press sheet. Be sure to observe postal regulations. This is a larger card, so it will cost more to mail it. Your local post office can supply you with a form showing the range of allowable proportions for cards if you want to wing it. The number of cards you make is up to you.

Paper: The postcards print on the same cover stock as the portfolio and brochure covers. When you pick your cover stock, remember that the *paper color itself* will be used as a color in this package, so pick a color of white that will work well as your "fourth color."

The stationery package

Measurements: The letterhead is a standard 8.5 × 11-inch sheet of stationery, and the envelope is a standard No. 10 business envelope, which measures 4.125 × 9.5-inches. We used a slightly oversize business card—3.5-inches wide and 2.25-inches tall, to accommodate a tall logo and lots of lines of type—but you can use the standard size of 3.5 × 2-inches if you wish (tall or wide, your choice). We also prefer oversize mailing labels; this one is 6-inches wide by 4-inches tall.

Paper: For the letterhead and envelope, pick a paper that matches your cover stock, above, in whiteness and brightness (don't try to pair a blue-white cover stock with a warm rosy stationery paper, for example). Keep the textures similar, too: Pair a "wove" (smooth) finish with a coated or calendered (smooth) cover stock. Twenty-five percent or more cotton fiber content in a writing paper says—and feels like—*quality*. The business card(s) will print along with the portfolio and brochure on heavy cover stock. For the mailing label, we recommend a "crack and peel" paper made especially for this purpose; again, match color and surface texture.

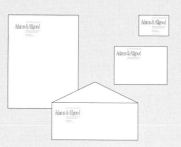

1   Start by making your logo

The heart of the portfolio design is a single, medium-weight font, uniformly applied to each piece. Select a font and set your name. Then begin with the business card: Scale your name to fit almost the full width of the card. Condense or expand the type as needed (within reason). If your name is very short, turn the card vertically.

Art   Art   Art
100%   80%   50%

If you extend it, stay within 120 to 130 percent. And with sans serif type, if vertical and horizontal stroke widths vary too much, you've stretched the type too far.

The stroke weights in this san serif logo are dangerously close to being too unequal.

The key is to set your name almost the full width of the business card. If your name is long and looks too small, condense the type somewhat. If it's very short and looks too big, expand it. As you do, pay attention to stroke weights: Serif fonts condense more gracefully than sans serifs (our eyes expect to see unequal stroke weights in a serif). But in sans serifs, stroke weights should be equal, or close to it.

2   Then add elements to make a signature

The signature is the visual unit of information, consisting of logo, address, phone number and other incidentals—that you'll repeat on each of the elements in the system.

Place your logo on the business card and center it left to right. Find a vertical axis in the name; we used an ampersand, but you could also select the first letter of the last name. Place your slogan, if any, above the logo, and place address, phone, fax and e-mail information below it. Put extra vertical space between groupings. Additional extra space, if any, should go above the logo.

TIP Use any font but *align on an axis*; that's what provides the *structure*.

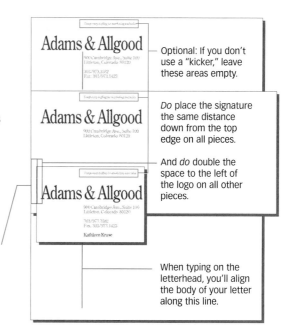

Options

Shift the axis left to right as needed to accommodate any logo length or orientation. If your name is more than two words, you can align on any word, but along the last proper name or most important word makes the most sense.

---

3 Lay out the stationery package

One of the coolest aspects of this portfolio is that the signature—your logo and related information—is identical in size and location on every piece. What could be simpler? The only modifications you'll make are to edit and use only the information critical to each piece: On the business card, use the company name, slogan, address, phone, fax and e-mail information, and your name and title. On the letterhead, remove your name and title; on the envelope and mailing label, remove those, plus the phone, fax and e-mail data.

Optional: If you don't use a "kicker," leave these areas empty.

Do place the signature the same distance down from the top edge on all pieces.

And *do* double the space to the left of the logo on all other pieces.

The business card is key: You designed it first because it's the smallest piece. On the letterhead and envelope, place the entire signature down from the top the same as on the business card, then slide it to the right to double the space to the left of the logo.

When typing on the letterhead, you'll align the body of your letter along this line.

Apply the logo as large as possible—without the rest of the signature—to the covers of the brochures, portfolios and cards.

TIP Don't measure the spaces around the logo; eyeball until they're visually equal.

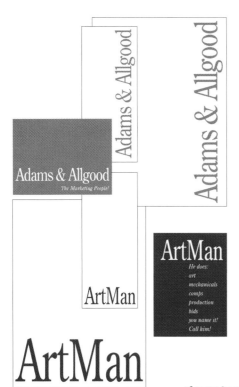

If your logo is long
Run it along the long edge of each piece. Give it about equal space at both ends and underneath the baseline. Here, we've used about a half inch. On the postcard, leave two or three times the space at the bottom for your message, which aligns along the axis like the signature.

If your logo is short
Run it along the short edge of each piece. Make it as big as you can—still with approximately equal space at the sides and bottom. The card can be laid out as above, or for a variation (bottom right) put the logo at the top and align a longer block of copy beneath it.

Color is what makes this whole package appealing. How do we get just three colors to look like a full palette?

Use *contrast* and *reverses* to get the most from this limited palette: The color of the paper itself contrasts with the ink colors and acts as a fourth color (white), which will reverse out of the background colors.

You'll also be printing *type* in the colors, so they must be dark enough in contrast to the paper color to "read." Select color values that are the equivalent of 50 percent gray or more. If in doubt, cut a sliver of the color and lay it on a sheet of white paper: How dark is it in comparison?

Distribute the colors: Use one for the logo, one for the body type, and one for the color swatch "linings"—the insides of the portfolio and brochure covers—and just for fun, the back of the business card.

NOTE PMS numbers refer to the Pantone® matching system. Colors shown are simulations only— they're what you get when you convert Pantone specs to process colors: Some are quite accurate, others are not so. Better check a Pantone® swatch book to get an accurate color.

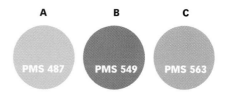

A   B   C

PMS 487 PMS 549 PMS 563

Muted spring palette

PMS 210 PMS 300 PMS 333

Bright spring palette

PMS 142 PMS 492 PMS 4725

Autumn palette

PMS WARM GRAY 6 PMS 287 PMS 208

Corporate palette

PMS 134 PMS 5473 PMS WARM GRAY 8

Forest palette

6 | Apply the color palette...

TIP When you print small type in a color, be sure it's dark enough to read.

Each piece in this system uses only one or two colors. When the individual one- and two-color pieces combine in the whole package, they make a handsome presentation. The white space looks clean and gives the solid colors a background to "pop" from. The large areas of solid color add depth and variety to the overall look.

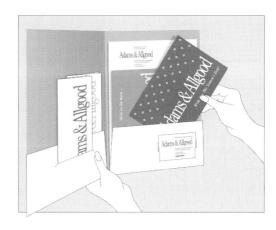

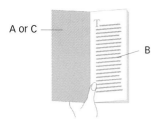

A or C

B

C

A

B

All of the text inside the brochure (and the logo on the front cover) prints in the B color (the darkest one in each palette). The inside cover is a solid swatch of either the A or C color—a nice contrast to the white text paper.

Each direct-mail card is one of the solid colors from the palette. All type and logos are reversed out in white. Type on the back side prints in the same color as the front—or all in the B color—on a white background.

7 | ...using contrast and reverses for punch

TIP Alternating every other line is visually distracting. Better to alternate colors by blocks of copy that make sense to group together.

Alternating colors and values—color on white, white on color—within each piece maximizes contrast and adds interest.

Temporary staffing for marketing and sales — A or C

Adams & Allgood — B

900 Cambridge Ave., Suite 100
Littleton, Colorado 80120 — A or C

303/973.3582
Fax: 303/973.1423

Kathleen Kruse ——— B

Alternate the B color with the next-darkest color in the palette (either A or C) when you apply color to the copy in the signature. The *smallest* type should be in the *darkest* color; the logo, which is large, can be in a somewhat lighter color.

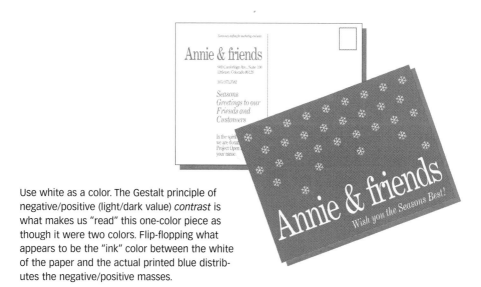

Use white as a color. The Gestalt principle of negative/positive (light/dark value) *contrast* is what makes us "read" this one-color piece as though it were two colors. Flip-flopping what appears to be the "ink" color between the white of the paper and the actual printed blue distributes the negative/positive masses.

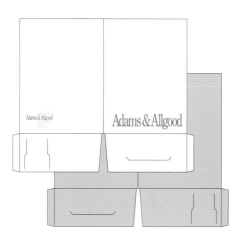

Use solid areas of color as *color swatches*—almost like liner papers—inside the portfolio and brochure covers, on the back of the business card, or wherever you have a blank panel where the punch of some solid color would look good. The luxurious use of lots of solid color makes this system attractive and gives it emotional appeal.

TIP Large blocks of color like this really make a big impact. Pick colors you love. Colors you love are colors you can *live with*; they express your own taste and style.

The brochure is a flexible format you can modify—it can have 4, 8 or 12 pages (or more)—to suit the length of your copy. And if you have more than one message or audience, you can create several brochures. The premise behind the brochure is that type can stand alone to make an attractive design. There are no photographs or illustrations. Instead, the same font used for the logo is repeated, smaller, for the body copy, and a decorative touch is added through the use of large "stick-up" initial caps that mimic the scale of the logo itself.

Make the overall brochure no larger than 4 × 9-inches so it fits inside a standard No. 10 business envelope.

Make the inside cover the A or C color, to contrast against the white paper of the text page opposite it.

Keep the front and back covers white, with just the logo and the signature in colored ink.

The inside pages are all copy. Print the text type in color to soften the look. Use the B color for both text and initial caps: It's the darkest one and will read best.

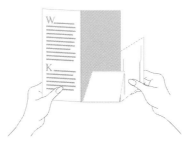

The unusual cover diecut shows up at the back of the brochure, where it reveals a folding flap pocket with a diecut slot for your business card.

The flap pocket is a handy place to tuck a cover letter, a product data sheet, or a price list. Note how the overlapping fold eliminates the need to glue the pocket. The entire inside of the cover prints in the A or C color.

Use one, two, or three sheets of text paper inside; each sheet yields four pages (two each side), for a total count of 4, 8 or 12 pages.

Keep the type simple. Use just one body text size and lead it deeply to keep it airy and readable. Use large initial caps for contrast and to emphasize a new point.

TIP When making several brochures, be consistent with the type size and leading. Accommodate length differences by varying the number of pages.

Start with the page proportions: A simple 3- or 4-pica margin surrounds the page equally on both sides and at the bottom (although you could "rag" the bottom margins to accommodate varying amounts of copy). The top margin should be two or three times greater.

Start the first paragraph with a "stick-up" initial but use no more than one per page. Make caps match the logo if you can: They should be four to six times larger than the body itself. Base-align the cap with the first line of text and indent the text to clear the right-hand serif or stem of the cap itself.

Set the body in either the same font as your logotype or in one that's similar. Start by sizing it 10 or 12 points, set solid. Then condense it to 90 to 95 percent wide, double the leading, and see how it fits the overall space. Adjust both size and leading until it fits your page limit. The exact combination of sizes isn't important; try for a ratio of leading approximately double the point size used.

Keep the copy all in one block by running paragraphs together, and use a dingbat to indicate the paragraph breaks. This yields a page with no visual interruptions. Left: We used a solid square from Zapf Dingbats, the same point size as the text but scaled 100 percent wide. Below: A more traditional dingbat would be the typographer's symbol for a paragraph—¶.

You've heard of clerical temps. You've probably heard of engineering, accounting and light industrial temps.

CENTURY OLD STYLE 10/10
100% WIDTH

You've heard of clerical temps. You've probably heard of engineer-

CENTURY OLD STYLE 10/20
90% WIDTH

Y ou've heard of clerical temps. You've probably heard of engineering, accounting, and light industrial temps. You may even have heard of legal, medical, and executive temps. But this may be the first time you've heard of a temporary employment firm specializing in marketing and sales temps. But why not? ■ Temporary employment offers many benefits to marketing and sales professionals like yourself: diversity, flexibility, income, the opportunity to establish contacts with a wide variety of firms, and even the opportunity to evaluate future employment possibilities. ■ Of course, added to the benefits of temporary work in general are the special benefits of working with Adams & Allgood. For one thing, we work only with sales and marketing personnel, so you always have our undivided attention. Our employees are recognized as marketing and sales professionals. ■ We have ongoing direct sales activities to assure a steady stream of

rate offered prior to your acceptance of a particular assignment. ¶ In addition to paying your wages and

Set off a ¶ in the same font as the text by making it bold and scaling it 120 percent wide, with an em space on each side.

This businesslike, you-are-there résumé presents the *person* behind
the stats.

How to design a modern résumé

What's the problem with an old, anonymous,
list-style résumé? It's that it puts the *person* in
the back of the bus while statistics, degrees and
titles do our driving. That's getting the cart
before the horse.

Real life is the other way around. We meet
the person, then hear about the accomplishments. That's the idea behind this very striking,
thoroughly modern résumé.

What sets this design apart is that the person
on the page looks real. The centerpiece silhouette gets the attention, yet what makes it work
is the layout. Here are the details.

Simplicity is key

Letter-size résumé (landscape orientation)
prints one side only, folds accordion style into
three equal panels and tucks into a No. 10
business envelope. This efficient design uses
only two typefaces—a light serif for text and
a bold sans serif for heads—and prints on
your office printer.

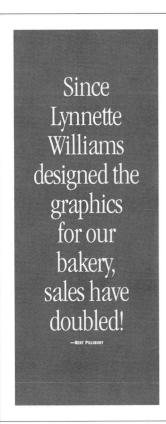

Since
Lynnette
Williams
designed the
graphics
for our
bakery,
sales have
doubled!

—BERT PILLSBURY

Add her design skills to your staff!

ACCOMPLISHMENTS Lorem ipsum dolor sit amet, consectetur adipscing elit, diam nonnumy eiusmod tempor incidunt ut labore et dolore magna aliquam erat volupat. Ut enim ad minimim veniami quis nostrud exercitation ulla laboris nonnumy eiusmod tempor incidunt uto labore et dolore magna aliquam erat volupat. Ut enim ad minimim veniami aliquip.

Her eye catching ads gave us a new upscale image.
—CLIFF MARTIN

SKILLS Duis autem vel eum irure dolor in reprehenderita in voluptate velit esse molestaie son consequat, vel illum dolore eu fugiate nullarod pariatur. At verote eos et accusamet justo odio dignissim qui blandit praesente lupatum delenit aiguena duos dolor et expedit distinct venia.

EDUCATION Tolestaier son consequat, vel illum dolore eu fugiat nulla pariatur. At verote eosa et accusam et justor odio dignissim qui blandit praesentae lup-

atum delenit aigue duos dolor et molestais exceptur sint occaecat cupidat non provident, simil tempor sunt in culpa qui officia deserunt mollit anim id est laborum eta dolor nam liber a tempor cum soluta nobis eligend optio comque.

EMPLOYMENT Temporeum eutem quinsud eta auir office debit aut tum rerum necessit atib saepe eveniet ut er repudiand sint et molestia quod maxim placeat facer omnis es voluptas assumenda est, omnis dolor repellendnon este recusand;possim omnis es voluptas assumenda est nesessit.

CURRENT JOB
1987–present. Duis autem velo eum irure dolor in reprehenderita in voluptate velit esse molestaie son consequat, vel illum dolore.

OLDER JOB
1985–1987. Duis autem vel eum irure dolor in reprehenderitas in voluptate velites esse molestaie son consequat, vel illum.

FIRST JOB
1984–1985. Duis autem vel eum irure dolor in reprehenderita in voluptate velit esse molestaie son consequat vela.

Lynnette
Williams

GRAPHIC DESIGNER

620 SANTA YNEZ WAY
APARTMENT 3
DALLAS, TEXAS 75207
(214) 555-5555

Page blueprint

Page setup: Letter size; landscape mode. Margins (in picas): Left, 2; Right, 2; Top, 8; Bottom, 2.

Column guides: Three columns, 3 picas between.

Ruler guides: Drag horizontal guides to 2, 4p6, 11p9, 33p8 and 36 picas from the top. Drag vertical guides 2, 23p8, 24p8, 28p8, 59 and 64 from the left side of the page.

Folds: (from the left) 22 and 44 picas.

Type: First panel headline quote: Garamond Light Condensed 44/44. Quote byline: Futura Condensed Extra Bold 7/9; small caps. Inside panel headline: Garamond Light Condensed 35/35. Inside panel quote: Garamond Light Condensed 16/16. Quote byline: Futura Condensed Extra Bold 5/8; small caps. Run-in subheads: Futura Condensed Extra Bold 10/12; set in lowercase small caps. Job listing sub-heads: Futura Condensed Bold 7/12. Text: Garamond

Light Condensed 10/12. Name: Garamond Light Condensed 22/23. Title: Futura Condensed Extra Bold 8/8; all caps. Address: Futura Condensed Bold 7/8; all caps.

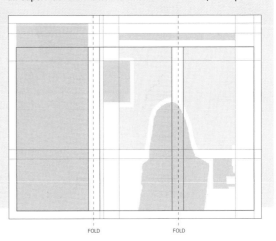

FOLD   FOLD

The success of this résumé depends on the photograph you use. The idea is to look like you do in person—well groomed, well dressed, businesslike, at ease. To appear most lifelike, the photo will be used in silhouette, so it should not be cropped above the waist. Dress in medium or dark colors; a plain white background is best.

A light background is easiest to silhouette. Have the photo taken in black and white, waist high, your body well within the frame so nothing is cropped out.

Create the silhouette. Use your favorite method to clip out the background. At low-res, you can probably use your page layout program's auto clipping. For high-resolution output, you should soften the edges with photo-retouching software.

Crop the silhouette to border's edge
To look like you're there in person, the silhouette ideally would bleed off the page. A standard office printer, however, will not print all the way to the edge. To get around this, create an artificial edge—a border—and crop to it instead.

The folding order dictates the format. The first panel is used for an introduction because it's seen separately when folded. Inside panels are combined into a single page, giving it an expansive look.

Inside text aligns with front panel headline. Alignment is neat; watch for opportunities.

Wide margins frame the story and look inviting. Keep reader attention with short line lengths. This not only looks more sophisticated, it makes your résumé appear brief and to the point.

A personal billboard
The front panel is ideal as a confident statement of ability or accomplishment. You might ask one of your references to write it for you, then paraphrase. Work carefully on the wording: The line between confidence and boasting is thin. Try variations and imagine how each would sound to someone else.

Center rules
between job listings. Hint: Position by eye, not by measurement.

facer omnis es voluptas assumenda es repellendnon este recusand:possim om assumenda est nesessit.

EMPLOYMENT. Temporeum eutem qu office debit aut tu rerum necessit atil ut er repudiand si et molestia quod r

CURRENT JOB s autem velo eum 1987–present. in voluptate velit esse renrehe at, vel illum dolore.

OLDER JOB 1985–1987. Duis autem vel eu in renrehenderitas in volunt

Layout's little organizers
When applying subheads in sizes similar to text, pick a font family with more than one bold weight. Type weight will separate information into levels of importance. Use the *extra bold* face for main section heads, and lighter *bold* for the job-listing subheads.

Build a setting for the mind, and words come alive.

Design a cover with background art

One of the designer's biggest jobs is to take plain words and bring them to life in the mind of the reader. But how do you bring to life a subject the reader cannot see, like a meeting? The answer is to *make it visible*. The most effective way to do so is with artwork.

To illustrate how, we made up a worst-case scenario: Design a black and white cover for a labor relations event that had no logo, no usable photos, no exotic locale, and a bureaucratic name.

In looking for clip art, you're not trying to illustrate the event literally. Instead, you want to borrow the *air* from the picture's visual imagery. The job of the picture is to create a feeling in the minds of readers that they'll assign to your event.

It's important, however, that words and picture be seamlessly integrated. The picture should not feel tacked on or incidental. Equally important, the picture must not be mistaken for the event. The best clip art for this is background art.

What follows are five excellent formats. Watch how the designs gently control the viewing levels and create harmony between what you read and what you feel.

The placard cover makes an *announcement*. When picking the main words—whether the event (below right) or the organization's name (right)—be prepared to live with them, because they look *official*. Reinforcing this effect is beautiful, old-style typography (Berkeley Oldstyle). The headline, all upper case, is artfully justified on a placard offset toward the top. Careful work is important here: Select a light-weight serif font, then pay attention to uniform letterspacing, line leading and margins. The descriptive text is justified, too. Note how the contrasting sans serif typeface brings ANNUAL MEETING quietly to the front.

A background of marble loans its quality to our event. This is key: We literally borrow its mental imagery. Marble is solid, enduring. It hints at the long halls of government.

When looking for a background, look for pictures that are low-contrast, with little detail, so the eye stays fixed on the words.

Finally, note the outer border matches the placard border. You may also choose other decorative lines such as triple or Scotch rules to carry the theme.

Stacking the text

Key to this look is beautiful typography, carefully justified, kerned and spaced. (**1**) Center the headline in independent, one- or two-word blocks, about half-page wide. (**2**) Adjust the point size of each line up or down until the text appears to justify, then equalize the leading between blocks. (**3**) Draw a rectangular placard evenly spaced around the headline, and (**4**) embellish the corners.

2   The magazine cover

Who'd guess this dramatic representation was for an annual meeting? This design takes advantage of the authority we tend to grant the media—that if it's published, it must be worth a look.

   Note the message the clip art sends. The image is tranquil; birds in flight suggest freedom from restraint. Both are fine qualities to associate with a labor relations meeting. It's important that your picture not be too definite—no celebrity faces, for example. In this format, it would be easy to mistake the picture for the event. Look for an image with large, open areas for nameplate and headlines.

Align headlines to nameplate
Nameplate in all caps S-P-A-N-S the top, evenly spaced from the sides (inset, upper right). Set headlines in a single text block aligned left, centered or right. Align the block with any portion of the nameplate or its subhead; its vertical position depends on the picture (right).

3   The gallery cover

A clean, restrained layout makes the picture do all of the work, ideal when your type library is uninspiring. A lightweight headline (here, 27 point) is anchored by a narrow black bar; descriptive text is small (10 point) and aligned to the last word in the head (inset), creating a vertical axis. The axis is emphasized by a tint.

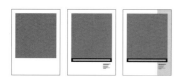

Picture first, then headline bar, type and tint.

The high-tech format is the most common in all of corporate designdom. A rigid grid system governs placement of both art and type (below left). Type is a single family, most commonly Helvetica; contrasts are made solely by differences in weight (note bold headline and light descriptive text). Picture and type never touch, so pictures are totally interchangeable. This quality is especially useful when you must design a unified series of covers—for a company's quarterly meetings, for example.

Specs
Page set-up: Portrait; **Dimensions:** 51 × 66 picas; **Margin in picas:** All 3p6; **Column guides:** Five columns with one pica between; **Type:** Headline 18/18 Helvetica Neue, 85 percent; Text 9/10 Helvetica Neue 45 with bold.

This treatment cleverly focuses the eye by *rescaling* the page—practically everything has been reduced to half its normal size (below). Note that the date and locale remain in a separate bar at the bottom; this important touch keeps the page looking big.

This is a surprisingly popular technique; you'll enjoy experimenting with it. Try first many kinds of cropping—tall and narrow, short and wide. Its effects on an image can be startling. Try, too, different placements—top, left, and bottom—and experiment with bleeds.

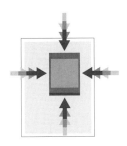

Note the type is carefully justified with the picture margins.

Sell! Visual organization turns an ordinary data sheet into a sales tool.

Make an easy-to-read data sheet

The humble data sheet is often a forgotten page. Problem is, it's often your first line of communication with the customer. It should be clear, organized and accessible. You don't want it showy, but the more organized the page, the better the impression you'll make: Just compare these two examples if you're not convinced. Here's how to make the best impression.

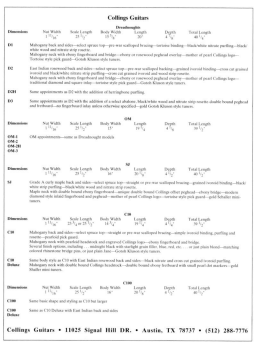

BEFORE

INSTRUMENT SPECIFICATIONS

DIMENSIONS

GUITAR STYLE	NUT WIDTH	SCALE LENGTH	BODY WIDTH	BODY LENGTH	BODY DEPTH	TOTAL LENGTH
Dreadnoughts (D)	1¹¹⁄₁₆"	25½"	15⅝"	20"	4⅞"	40¼"
Orchestra Model (OM)	1¹¹⁄₁₆"	25½"	15"	19¼"	4⅛"	39½"
Small Jumbo (SJ)	1¹¹⁄₁₆"	25½"	16"	20⅛"	4½"	40½"
C10	1¹¹⁄₁₆"	23¾" or 25½"	14¾"	19¼"	4¼"	39½"
C100	1¹¹⁄₁₆"	25½"	16"	20⅛"	4½"	40½"

APPOINTMENTS

MODEL(S)

D1/OM1

BODY—Mahogany back and sides • Select spruce top • Tortoise binding • Prewar scalloped bracing • Black/white nitrate purfling • Black/white wood and nitrate strip rosette • Tortoise style pick guard. **NECK**—Mahogany neck with ebony fingerboard and bridge • Ebony or rosewood peghead overlay • Mother-of-pearl Collings logo • Gotoh Kluson style tuners.

D2/OM2

BODY—East Indian rosewood back and sides • Select spruce top • Grained ivoroid binding • Prewar scalloped backing • Cross cut grained ivoroid and black/white nitrate strip purfling • Crosscut grained ivoroid and wood strip rosette • Tortoise style pick guard. **NECK**—Mother-of-pearl Collings logo • Mahogany neck with ebony fingerboard and bridge • Ebony or rosewood peghead overlay • Traditional diamond-and-square inlay • Gotoh Kluson style tuners.

D2H/OM2H

Same appointments as D2/OM2 with the addition of herringbone purfling.

D3/OM3

Same appointments as D2/OM2 with the addition of a select abalone, black/white wood and nitrate strip rosette double-bound peghead and fretboard • No fingerboard inlay unless otherwise specified • Gold Gotoh Kluson style tuners.

SJ

BODY—Grade A curly maple back and sides • Select spruce top • Straight or prewar scalloped bracing • Grained ivoroid binding • Black/white strip purfling • Black/white wood and nitrate strip rosette • Tortoise style pick guard. **NECK**—Maple neck with double-bound ebony fingerboard • Unique double-bound Collings offset peghead • Ebony bridge • Mother-of-pearl Collings logo • Modern diamond style inlaid fingerboard and peghead • Gold Schaller mini-tuners.

C10

BODY—Mahogany back and sides • Select spruce top • Straight or prewar scalloped bracing • Simple ivoroid binding, purfling and rosette • Pearloid pick guard. **NECK**—Mahogany neck with pearloid headstock and engraved Collings logo • Ebony fingerboard and bridge. **FINISH**—Several finish options, including . . . midnight black with starlight grain filler, blue, red, etc. . . . or just plain blond • Matching colored rhinestone bridge pins, or just plain Jane • Gotoh Kluson style tuners.

C10 Deluxe

BODY—Same body style as C10 with East Indian rosewood back and sides • Black nitrate and crosscut grained ivoroid purfling. **NECK**—Mahogany neck with double-bound Collings headstock • Double-bound ebony fretboard with small pearl dot markers • Gold Shaller mini-tuners.

C100

Same basic shape and styling as C10 but larger.

C100 Deluxe

Same as C10 Deluxe with East Indian back and sides.

Collings
GUITARS
11025 SIGNAL HILL DRIVE
AUSTIN, TEXAS 78737 ♦ (512) 288-7776

AFTER

Organize, organize, organize!

The goal of a data sheet is to showcase facts for speedy reference. This is not possible if there is no coherent order to the data you are presenting. It should go without saying, but before you begin your layout, read the copy. If you don't understand the terminology, find someone to explain it to you. You'll need a working knowledge to determine how the information should be arranged. Some suggestions:

Page setup
The single grid gives the illusion of two by using a hanging indent.
Page setup: Portrait mode; Margins in picas: Left 6p4; Right, 9p4; Top, 9p4; Bottom, 6p4. **Ruler guides:** Horizontal guides 2p6 and 8 picas from top. Vertical guide 15p4 from the left side of the page.
Type: Headline: Times Ten Roman 19.5/19.5. Subheads: Helvetica 95 Black 8/10. Chart subheads: Helvetica 85 Heavy 6.5/6.5. Text: Times Ten Roman 9/10.5. **Paragraphs:** Left indent, 9; First indent, –9.

White space beckons the reader

Wall-to-wall text is as tiresome as the party blabbermouth. Wide margins relax and beckon the reader in.

Group similar types of information

The original data sheet scattered guitar dimensions all over the page. Combining them into a single chart creates a focal point—an important characteristic of good design—and an aid for product comparisons.

Define categories

Large chunks of information will overwhelm and put off the reader, so look for ways to break the data into categories. In our case, we divided the page into two main sections: dimensions and appointments. The lower section was further divided by style, model and component. To each of these parts you *must* then…

Add headlines

Headlines and subheads are critical flags that signal what is to come. Use these markers to guide the reader to the data. Lack of subheads is one reason the original data sheet is confusing.

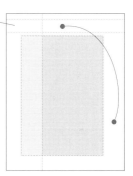

Text is pushed left to make a dynamic asymmetrical layout. Note that the top and right margins are equal, as are the left and bottom.

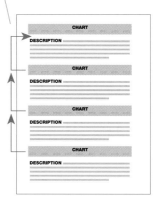

Anchor your charts horizontally

For a sleek chart, the fewer vertical lines the better. Tab stops create the vertical alignment. The head is set off only by a tint.

Use run-in subheads and bullets to organize

Contrasting, run-in subheads effectively separate data that's in paragraph form. Isolate single items with eye-stopping bullets.

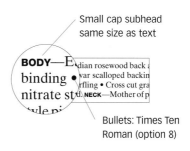

Small cap subhead same size as text

Bullets: Times Ten Roman (option 8)

Create hierarchy for easy reading

Hierarchy is the viewing order the designer establishes to make a page easy to read. This is done by varying the size and weight of the elements. Items to be seen first should be large, bold or placed within a tint box. Keep less important information smaller and lighter in value (no tint box). Hierarchy gives your page direction because the eye sees from large to small, bold to light.

Note how the dark-to-light progression leads the eye down the page.

Your eye follows the descending order of size and weight in the fonts at left. Hierarchy makes the data easier to find.

Watch for alignment opportunities

A visually organized page is well aligned. To achieve this, you'll typically key on the focal point—in our case, it's the chart. Note how most of the page aligns with the first tab stop. Watch for similar opportunities.

Text should align with text. If your chart has a background tint, extend both tint and rules into the margin.

On a form, function is *everything.* Here are the simple rules.

How to improve every form you make

The best form in the world is the one people like to use. It's clear, easy to read and has plenty of room to fill it in. It's hard to overestimate the value of such a form. A poorly designed form can easily impede business both inside and outside an organization.

On a form, function is everything.

There are two basic kinds of forms: *informational,* used to collect data; and *analytical,* used to track, manipulate, calculate or store data. One form may be both.

In designing a form, pay attention to sequence. This starts by first grouping the information into large sections, *titleplate, identifier, body* and *routing,* then presenting the details in a way that makes the information easy to understand, easy to fill in and—every bit as important—*easy to retrieve.* A design that encourages timely, error-free responses will give you a great reputation for meeting your company's communication needs.

Here's how to do it.

WHAT'S ON A FORM?

A form is a carrier that moves information through a company's unique read-write-transmit-process-route-retrieve-and-file circuit. *It must fit this circuit.* Before designing a thing, take the time to learn how its information will be used by Jill, Bob, Ted—everyone who touches it—department by department.

Assign your data to the four major sections
Read through the copy, and answer:
1. Whose form is it and what is it for? (**1 titleplate**)
2. Who's filling it out? (**2 identifier**)
3. What do we want to know or disseminate? (**3 body**)
4. Who processes it, and how? (**4 routing**)
Sift your data thoroughly and assign every bit of information to a section. Don't leave any out.

Rough out a page
- Stick to the subject within each section; don't put product information in a people section.
- Place information *in sequence.* The sales department, for example, may handle the form before accounting. A ZIP code normally appears after the state. Don't substitute a fax number and move the ZIP up a line or you'll confuse everyone. *The most common error in form design is to place information out of sequence just because it fits.*
- Complete one section before moving to the next.
- Signal clearly when the subject changes. Errors are made when thought processes collide.

MAJOR SECTIONS

1. Titleplate
You. Your company name, address and the form's title. Sometimes a date.

2. Identifier
Them. The name, address, phone, codes, whatever that identify the person or company filling in the form.

3. Data collector or body
The heart of the form. The section where questions are asked, products are ordered, and so forth. Forms experts refer to this process as "capturing" information.

4. Verification, routing
Accommodates approval or validation signatures. Can also contain routing instructions and other miscellany.

PARTS

Fill-in highlighter
Tints to emphasize important fill-in fields

Form number
For revision control, filing and so forth.

Fill-in fields
Areas between the lines for filling in

Captions
The tiny, label-like words that ask questions

Subheads
Identify sections

Column headings
Identify columns

Rules
Dividers. Different weights for different things.

Fill-in aids
Dollar signs and other symbols reduce manual fill-in

Check-box fill-ins
Minimize fill-in time, ensure uniform answers

Instructions
Eliminate confusion and speed fill-in by putting instructions adjacent to their corresponding fill-ins

Small print
Things like condition statements. Can be put on the back, in which case they're called "backers."

XAMPLEX ✪

Corporate Headquarters
555 American Plaza
Chicago, IL 55555
312.555.5555
Fax: 312.555.5556

FORM #331100

MAIL ORDER FORM

NAME   CUSTOMER CODE (FROM MAIL LABEL)

COMPANY

ADDRESS   SUITE #

CITY   STATE   ZIP

DAY PHONE   EVENING PHONE   FAX

Merchandise Ordered

QUANTITY	ITEM NUMBER	PRODUCT DESCRIPTION	UNIT PRICE	EXTENDED PRICE
			$	$
			$	$
			$	$
			$	$
			$	$
			$	$
			$	$
			$	$
			$	$
			$	$

SUBTOTAL $

SALES TAX   CA residents only $

Method of Payment

☐ Check   ☐ Money order   ☐ Visa

☐ MasterCard   ☐ American Express   ☐ Discover

CREDIT CARD OR CHECK NUMBER   EXPIRATION DATE

SIGNATURE

SHIPPING
Domestic orders: $4.00. Hawaii and Alaska: $8.00. International orders: 25% of total order amount for Airmail or 10% of total (minimum $15.00) for surface. Federal Express: Economy Service (2 day) $7.00. Standard Overnight: $12.00. Priority Overnight: $19.00. Hawaii and Alaska add $10.00 to above charges. International: Fax for quote.

SHIPPING $

TOTAL $

Notice: XAMPLEX shall not be held liable for any direct or indirect loss or damage resulting from use or misuse of these products, even if XAMPLEX has been advised of the possibility of such damages. All prices subject to change without notice. XAMPLEX is not responsible for typographical errors. Delivery dates depend on availability of products. **Exchanges and Returns:** A restocking fee may apply to returned merchandise (non-Shareware) in salable condition. Please call 1.312.555.5555 for return approval. For CD-ROM drive returns or warrantied repairs please use extension X. **Tech Support/Information:** If you have questions before ordering, please call our information number 1.312.555.4444. Note: Operators at the toll-free number are not equipped to answer all technical questions. For questions or help using PD/Shareware disks please refer to XAMPLEX's Get Info newsletter or our Software Encyclopedia.

1 Design a titleplate

If the public will see your form, an attractive titleplate is as valuable as your business card. The titleplate is where you add style. It identifies your company and names the form. Include your logo, name, address and usually all phone and fax numbers. Form numbers and dates can also go here. If your company has an existing "look," use it on your titleplates. If not, here are some suggestions:

Big name

Here the company name, logo and address block form a neat, carefully spaced triangle whose visual weight is offset completely by the empty field of white. Note the points of alignment: The company name is flush with the data fields, and the circular logo is *in the margin*, sized to match the name. The address block aligns *left* along the line created by the logo, the same distance from the logo that the name is. In spite of its size, the company name speaks softly in a gray tint. "Mail Order Form" title is small but amply visible alone in the empty space.

Long name

Here a long name aligns to a wide left margin. Gray underscore links name to distant logo and address block. Underscore lassos the logo by stopping at its right-hand edge.

The data

A form holds two categories of data: static and dynamic. Static data is the information you design. Dynamic data is what the customer fills in.

Static data   Dynamic data

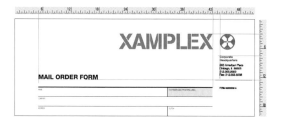

Specs
Logo: 3p3 diameter; **Company:** AG Book Stencil 54/54-pt (Helvetica Bold or Black would substitute nicely); **Address, phone:** Helvetica Condensed Light with Condensed Bold 7.5/8.5-pt; **Form Title:** AG Book Stencil 16/16-pt

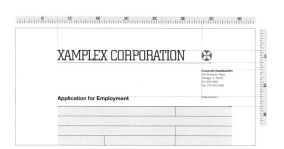

Specs
Logo: 2p3 diameter; **Company:** Berthold City Light 36/36-pt; **Line:** 50K 3-pt rule; **Address, phone:** Helvetica Neue Light with Bold 7.5/9-pt; **Form Title:** Helvetica Neue Bold 14/14-pt

Big title

Here the prominent title, address block and logo all hang from the top margin; the logo hovers above the wide, empty space.

Specs
Logo: 3p4 diameter; **Company:** Helvetica Neue Bold 7/9-pt, all caps; **Address, phone:** Helvetica Neue Light with Bold 7/9-pt; **Form Title:** Helvetica Compressed 26/26-pt

---

2   The steps to perfect form layout

Keep four goals in mind: ease of data entry, ease of data retrieval, error reduction and *people's willingness to use the form.*

Set wide outside margins

White space makes a page inviting
Form data is typically jammed wall to wall in a dense, weary mass, but spacious white margins yield the same benefit on a form that they do on a newsletter page. They impart a sense of airiness that makes the form seem easy to deal with. This is key when you're asking a reader to respond to you. Start with one-inch margins on all sides, then add more for physical conditions: Will the form be filled out on a clipboard? Add a half-inch on the top. Placed in a binder? Filed horizontally? Add a half-inch on the left. A wide margin can also be used strictly for aesthetics. In the case above right, a wide *right* margin accommodates the titleplate design. Wide margins have another benefit: They make the completed form easier to read.

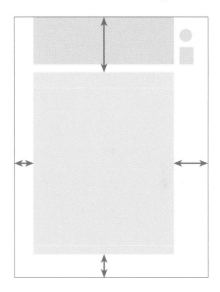

If a form will be filled out on a clipboard, leave an extra 1-half inch of space at the top.

Use uniform line spacing

Design for various completion methods

Some people still do use typewriters to fill in forms, and many others fill them in by hand. So design your forms with even, standard typewriter double spacing, which means 24 point, or 2 picas between lines. So a typist can roll the form to its starting point without adjusting the paper, count down in 2-pica increments from the top of the *sheet* to your first fill-in field.

When an oddball heading, subhead or caption throws off the interval, jimmy its leading (left) so the next fill-in field remains correct. Most typewriters can also type at space-and-a-half, or 18-point intervals, but that's a bit tight for handwriting.

Align fill-in fields vertically

Space for tab stops

A form is easy to fill in if a typist can jump to tab stops rather than having to space over. Divide your page into columns (eight is typical; fewer is better) and start every fill-in field on a column. Be strict about it.

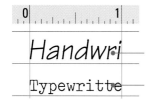

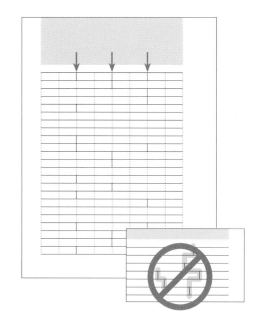

How much space do they need? A monospacing typewriter sets 10 or 12 characters, including spaces and punctuation, per inch; a proportional-spacing typewriter sets about 12. Handwriting can fit any space, but the comfortable average is seven characters per inch. Err on the side of too much space.

Divide sections with uniform rules

Three line weights always work

Rules serve two functions on a form: They divide and categorize *kinds* of information. Use 2-pt. rules to set off major sections (A). Use 1-pt. rules to subdivide sections (B). Use 0.25-pt. rules to separate individual lines (C). For special emphasis, fill a field with light gray (D).

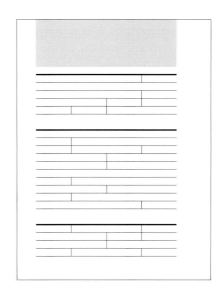

---

3 Set sleek, efficient type

Use sans serif typestyles

Forms by nature appear busy, even cluttered. To minimize this busyness, set forms in sans serif typefaces. Their sleek, mechanical appearance is generally easier to read in small sizes, and prints cleaner—especially on laser printers—than serif type. Set captions in all caps (top), which are more uniform than lowercase. You'll be surprised by how small they should be: Since you want captions to recede once the form is filled in, use 5- to 7-point type, in light and medium weight. If you're limited on choices, subdue a heavier weight with a gray tint (bottom). For subheads and section heads, use bold.

ADDRESS
123 Oak St.
Sans-serif

ADDRESS
123 Oak St.
Serif

ADDRESS
123 Oak St.

Tuck captions into upper-left corners

We read left to right, top to bottom, so no rule in form design is more rigid than this one: Set captions neatly in the upper-left corners of their fill-in fields, but beside, not below, not in the middle. This leaves the entire field, not just a portion, available for fill in. Another benefit: A typist can set tab stops. There's no need to space over to each starting point, because fill-in always begins at the same place no matter how long the caption.

Name (Last, First, Middle) *Conklin, Alicia,*

NAME (LAST, FIRST, MIDDLE)
Conklin, Alicia, Lynnette

Provide multiple-choice check boxes

Since it's easier to check a box than write an essay, the more multiple-choice answers your form has, the better the response will be. The uniformity of the check boxes has another benefit: It makes retrieval a breeze (no hand-writing to decipher). Set the first checkbox on the baseline about a spacebar's distance before its answer, then set the following box at the next tab stop. Maintain at least an em space between entries so it's clear which box belongs to which.

HOW LONG HAVE YOU LIVED AT THIS ADDRESS?

☐ 1 YEAR   ☐ 2 YEARS   ☐ 3 YEARS

Less space here than here

Box and text height should be about the same.

☐ 1 YE

For survey forms you should always provide multiple choice answers, at least if you want a response. They are easy to fill in, and—most important—return predictable, uniform answers that are easy to process. Stack questions in boxed sections, and put one pica between lines to match single-space typing.

4 | Repeat the format on all your forms

Think modular

Your company's forms are seen and handled more often than any other documents; you want them to look and act as much alike as possible. Use the same titleplace from form to

form, and repeat margin widths, spacing, line weights, type styles, weights and sizes. If you can, use the same tab settings. Whenever possible, repeat entire sections, such as the ID field (left) from form to form.

Forms are also an important part of a corporate business image. They serve daily as your silent representatives. The orderly structure and appearance of your forms will go a long way to conveying to the public your company's organized, efficient methods.

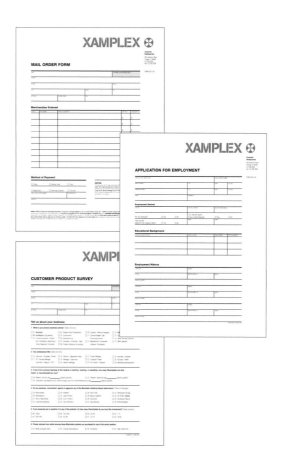

5 | Finish with the small print

Transactions on many forms must be approved or at least verified. When the approval pertains to the entire form, it should be located at the end of the form. When the approval pertains to only one section, it should be part of that section. Include space for a signature, date, and if you have one, a qualifying statement. Set small print like this about 2 points larger than caption size, then float it—it won't fit the grid—in an open field.

> I certify that the information shown on this application is true
> as it considers necessary to evaluate my qualifications for em
> which includes a drug test, at Company expense may be requi
> will be grounds for discharge from employment
>
> SIGNATURE

Index

The look and function of everything we see benefits from design. Subscribe to Before & After, the how-to magazine for visual communicators!

If you like what you found in this book, you'll love Before & After magazine. Each issue is packed with powerful solutions to improve the visual impact of your communication materials. There is no other design resource like Before & After magazine. Before & After magazine will show you, step-by-step, how to apply design principles and make the best design decisions for your project. With Before & After magazine, you will:

- Learn the techniques of better visual communication
- Understand why things look the way they do
- Find inspiration and fresh ideas
- Discover tips for creating professional visual techniques

Subscribe online at www.bamagazine.com